THE TRUE STORY OF
SAINT BERNADETTE

THE TRUE STORY OF SAINT BERNADETTE

BY

Fr. HENRY PETITOT, O.P.

TRANSLATED BY

A BENEDICTINE OF STANBROOK ABBEY

THE NEWMAN PRESS

WESTMINSTER, MARYLAND

CVM PERMISSV SVPERIORVM O.S.B.

NIHIL OBSTAT : JOANNES P. CAN. ARENDZEN, D.D., PH.D., M.A.

CENSOR DEPVTATVS

IMPRIMATVR : E. MORROGH BERNARD

VICARIVS GENERALIS

WESTMONASTERII : DIE XXVII APRILIS MCMXLIX

PRINTED IN GREAT BRITAIN AT
THE UNIVERSITY PRESS, ABERDEEN, FOR
THE NEWMAN PRESS, WESTMINSTER, MARYLAND

First published 1950

CONTENTS

FOREWORD

•

BERNADETTE is a very great saint. We are not sufficiently aware of it. The few months which she spent at the home of her foster-mother, looking after the sheep, have left in the mind of the public the picture of a mere shepherdess, ingenuous but an ignoramus.

We consider, on the contrary, that, without ever having become what in our day is called an 'intellectual,' Bernadette's mind was widely open to spiritual and supernatural truths, and that throughout her life she made progress in the knowledge of the Catholic religion. Moreover, she patiently practised all the virtues that lead to sanctity. From this standpoint we have no hesitation in saying that she is a great model, and that her canonization will effectually contribute to the development of the revival of religion in our time.

If we except the revelations which have contributed to found the Lourdes pilgrimage, Bernadette seems to us the simplest saint known to the Catholic Church. She is, indeed, still more simple than St. Teresa of the Child Jesus. She did not precisely practise, still less did she teach, a particular doctrine, be it even the Way of Spiritual Childhood. Her entire spiritual and religious life offers no outstanding instance of exceptional graces, miracles or visions. From this point of view, again, she is truly of our time. Nevertheless, those who will attentively ponder her conduct, her words, the few thoughts, resolutions and prayers which she wrote, will there find some very precious lessons which will provide them with a powerful source of strength in trials. The humble Bernadette, among all the saints, is one of those who will best teach us how to suffer in soul and body with a patience and piety which will make us conformable to our divine Master.

CHAPTER I

Bernadette Before the Apparitions

WHEN beginning to treat of Bernadette, Père Cros makes this reflection which is psychologically and theologically quite exact. ' God requires from, or confers upon, those members of the human family whom He sees fit to use as instruments some corresponding aptitude, some proportion, apparent or hidden, between them and the end He has purposed ; but what stands out, what leaps to the eye, is the weakness, the littleness, the poverty, the limitations and multiple disproportion of the chosen instruments. St. Bernardine of Siena, in a Latin period which it is almost impossible to translate, expresses the same thought in a still more striking manner : " It is a general rule that when divine grace destines a person to an exceptional vocation, it confers upon him the gifts that are necessary to his state, and which ennoble the recipient in a special manner ". ' [1]

For the majority of those who live constantly with these privileged souls, those gifts often pass unnoticed. Their contemporaries look only on the surface : at the outward weaknesses, the littleness, the human failings, the limitations which, as says Père Cros, leap to the eye. The true, interior, hidden greatness escapes them. One of the Franciscans of the first generation, Jordan of Giano, who went on the German mission and there exercised a very fruitful apostolate, towards the close of his life, dictated a chronicle wherein he recalled the story of this journey. He ingenuously acknowledges the small esteem in which

[1] Sermon on St. Joseph.

he held the person of St. Francis when he knew him. He did not consider him a man of outstanding holiness ; he saw that he was full of human weaknesses, and he confesses that his absolute veneration for him dated only from his canonization. 'This candid acknowledgement,' writes Fr. Cuthbert, 'explains many things to the generations who did not know Francis when he belonged to this world.' [1]

We might generalize, and suggest that it has been thus with a number of saints, and that they were absolutely unrecognized for such by those who knew them at close quarters, and seemed best placed for knowing them well. If any priest—and he was both intelligent and zealous—should have known the Curé of Ars, it was his curate, the Abbé Raymond ; but the latter thought only of supplanting M. Vianney. He considered that he was sometimes excitably 'worked up,' and that many things in the parochial administration were defective. He tried the Saint's patience in strange ways, and the latter even wrote to his bishop, asking him to change the curate, but tore up the letter at the last moment. The Abbé Raymond was persuaded that the Curé had a special affection for him and could not do without him.

In his book, *The Psychology of the Saints*, M. Emile Joly writes : ' No man is a hero to his valet, but the saint is never more appreciated than by his intimates and those who see him close at hand.' This opinion can be accepted only with many reserves. St. John of the Cross was considered a man below the average by his own brethren. St. Teresa of Lisieux was unrecognized by the majority of the nuns of her community. Let us not be surprised that Bernadette, likewise, was unknown during her lifetime by a number of persons who ' knew ' her well, or even lived with her

[1] *Life of St. Francis*, by Fr. Cuthbert, O.F.M.

for years. It is still less surprising that writers who rely upon outward happenings, without thoroughly examining the subject, should have passed judgements upon Bernadette and her family which are, at least partially, erroneous.

It must not be forgotten that Bernadette's parents, whose poverty and destitution are insisted upon in realistic fashion, and who were, indeed for several years, the most wretchedly situated inhabitants of Lourdes, had previously known, throughout their youth, very comfortable circumstances; and that they had been reared in principles of right living quite frequently met with among the lower middle-class in country districts. When we bear in mind this early up-bringing, we are less surprised at what was remarked later by Sister Eléonore Cassagnes, Secretary General of the Sisters of Nevers : ' It could be seen that she had received a training superior to her birth. No one would have thought that she came from so lowly a station as she did.' We must not lose sight of the fact, therefore, that Bernadette, as well as her parents, had known what it meant to be well off ere they fell into the blackest destitution. This explains many things. Louise Casterot, her mother, liked cleanliness ; she brought up her children well ; family prayers were said ; all went to church. André Sajoux, the cousin who occupied the upper floor of the *cachot* where the whole Subirous family lived in one room, bears witness that neither the mother nor the children ever begged. ' They would rather have starved to death.' They belonged to the ' shame-faced poor.'

Bernadette, the eldest of the family, born on January 7, 1844, was obviously not a saint from childhood, and in this work it is precisely our intention to follow her moral progress, step by step from the beginning, as closely as possible, as she rose to sanctity.

As a child, a noteworthy characteristic of Bernadette was her anxiety about upright conduct, and even her premature concern to practise virtue and make others do so. Her cousin, Jeanne Védère, who subsequently became a Trappist Cistercian nun in the monastery of Blagnac, remembered a significant detail. When her parents were still living at the Boly mill, Bernadette's mother was in the habit of keeping open house for their customers, and often spent more on them than she received ; it was an obvious abuse. Bernadette was not more than ten years old when she deplored this bad management, as did Jeanne Védère. One day she asked her cousin to speak about it to her parents. ' Needless to say,' says Jeanne, ' I did not undertake to do so. The first time I returned to Lourdes, I gathered that Bernadette had told them that I disapproved of this custom, for my aunt said to me : " You must be surprised always to find women eating here, but we cannot do otherwise. It is the custom at Lourdes." ' [1] Young as she was, had it depended upon herself only, Bernadette would have acted otherwise than according to custom, and perhaps have saved her parents from the ruin for which they were heading.

It was shortly afterwards, in 1857, that she was sent to Bartrès, where she remained only some months. The details of her sojourn there are well known. Her foster-mother, Marie Aravant, had asked for her to look after her children, and she had also promised to send her to the catechism class, but she made use of her chiefly as shepherdess to a small flock of sheep. ' They made her look after them nearly every day,' says the maid, Jeanne-Marie Garros. ' She was well

[1] *Bernadette et Jeanne Védère.*   Notes intimes, p. 42.

treated and loved by nearly all, but especially by
Aravant himself, an excellent man. We were good
friends,' she adds, ' and never quarrelled ; on the
contrary, she was so good ! I never noticed a fault
in her. In spite of the weariness caused by her short,
laboured breathing, she was always bright and merry
and never complained about anything or anybody.
She obeyed everyone, she did not answer back, she
took what was given her and showed herself pleased.'
As regards these good qualities, the foster-mother's
account agrees with that of the servant.

Jeanne-Marie Garros tells us that Bernadette was
well treated and liked by nearly everybody. This
reserve, this *nearly*, raises a little problem which is not
usually solved by the biographers of the Saint. One
of the Brothers of the Christian Schools of Lourdes
writes : ' The little consideration shown her subsequently at Bartrès made her understand that they
were already tired of her.' Whence came this want
of consideration ? It has been supposed that Aravant
was a hard, selfish man and sometimes treated her
badly. The truth is quite otherwise, and we can
learn it from Jeanne Védère, who was in Bernadette's
confidence. 'One day, when I was with her, a priest
stopped us and spoke familiarly with her. When he
had gone, I asked her who this priest was. " He is a
relation of my foster-mother," she replied ; " he is so
kind ; I like him very much. He always took my
part when I was at Bartrès and he was in the house.
My foster-mother was not always pleasant. When
this priest used to come in holiday time, he was more
friendly with me than with the other children; so
after M. l'Abbé had made some remarks to her my
foster-mother changed her manner whilst he was in
the house . . . but after he had gone she behaved
as usual again." '

During the later days of her stay at Bartrès, Bernadette was unhappy and wished to return to her family. ' But, since you were not comfortable, why did you not tell your father ? ' asked her cousin. ' Oh no,' answered Bernadette, ' I was thinking how God willed it. When one thinks : " *the good God is allowing it*," one does not complain.' ' It upset me,' adds Jeanne Védère, ' to hear her. I had not the courage to ask her what her foster-mother did to her.' [1]

So after her cousin had confided in her, Jeanne Védère felt her heart so full that she did not try to learn more of the facts ! It must be remembered that Bernadette had been nursed by Marie Aravant, after the latter had lost her first-born infant ; hence she had been treated as a child of the house. Marie Aravant retained a great affection for her and invited her to Bartrès every year for the feast of St. John the Baptist and for the carnival. During these few days, Bernadette was feasted and petted by her foster-mother. In 1857, however, when Bernadette stayed there for four months, Marie Aravant had eight children of her own. Naturally, her affections were engaged. Little by little, she tired of Bernadette and failed to show her the thoughtful, motherly attentions to which she had been accustomed. The latter was treated like a servant and even rather like a stranger. She was even treated unkindly, since the Abbé Aravant had to defend her more than once when he was in the house. As we shall see later, under a somewhat cold exterior Bernadette was by nature very sensitive and affectionate. At fourteen, that age when a girl is wont to give her affection generously, she must have suffered more than might have been thought when she was constantly made aware of the difference between her foster-mother's past and

[1] *Bernadette et Jeanne Védère.* Notes intimes, p. 40.

present treatment of her. She was beginning to learn by hard experience how fickle is human affection. Later she was to suffer still more. The poignant trials which she experienced at Bartrès, in December 1857, would never have decided her to return home, for she was already convinced of a capital supernatural truth which, by instinct and by a gift of God, she was already practising with a kind of heroism, and which she explained so clearly. We shall find this principle very often later on, and she observed it until her death : To conform one's will to the will of God, and to be patient under trials is the way to become a saint.

Thinking over this truth and Bernadette's conduct, we are not astonished that the Abbé Ader, who carried out the duties of parish priest at Bartrès and was very pious, said as he watched her lead her flock and noted the girl's candour and innocence : 'The children to whom the Blessed Virgin appeared on the mountain of La Salette must have been like that little girl.'

Over and beyond her moral trial, Bernadette was beginning to suffer physically all the time. From the age of six, her mother had noticed in her a bronchial weakness which rendered her breathing difficult. In 1854, aged ten, after an attack of cholera, she became asthmatic. Jean-Baptist Estrade tells us that she grew up with difficulty, and remained weak and ailing. 'Her little chest was oppressed owing to an obstinate, asthmatic condition, and when afflicted with paroxysms of coughing, she was suffocated and fell into long and disquieting fainting fits. This trouble was caused by tuberculosis which was to spread through her body, rendering her more delicate still, and make her suffer in all kinds of ways until her death.' Well may Père Cros say : 'To other preparations, God willed to add that of suffering, and to set the seal of the Cross definitely upon this chosen soul.'

Notwithstanding, Bernadette was not at all gloomy. All the witnesses are agreed in stating that she was pleasant, lively, merry ; that she enjoyed herself thoroughly with her companions. Reticent when it was a question of supernatural favours and spiritual matters, she was a fluent and easy talker in her patois, and in familiar conversation she was lively and witty. Just before the apparitions, she was thus described by those who knew her : ' She was a girl,' writes the local schoolmaster, ' small for her age, with a charming face, rather browned and with fresh colour, and an expression of perfect peace of mind, sincerity and innocence.' Jean-Baptist likewise relates : ' Bernadette looked about ten or eleven years of age. Her face was fresh coloured and round ; her expression one of great sweetness and simplicity, the tone of her voice, though a little strident, was pleasing. She wore a white hood (*capulet*) and without being sumptuous her other clothes were clean and in good condition.' The *Procureur Impérial* was to speak likewise when he made Bernadette appear before him for the first time. ' There was no pretension in her dress, which was irreproachably clean, witnessing to self-respect and dignity in her poverty. Her head covering was a sort of muslin of which the coloured pattern was almost obliterated by frequent washings, and half covered her head, pressing down the hair so tightly as to leave only the clear outline of the skull. Suffering from a bronchial ailment, the poor child seemed to breathe with still more difficulty beneath the shapeless, heavy jacket meant to protect her. When she spoke in her simple language, her gentle and convinced tone inspired confidence. When she expressed a noble idea or something out of the common, there came over her features a gentle and penetrating charm which was only the outward overflowing of an innocent soul.' What the functionary does not tell us, and what was noticed by all, was the sweetness and often striking expression of her great brown eyes.

A month before the apparitions, Bernadette felt strongly urged interiorly by an ardent longing to make her first Communion. Privileged souls have mysterious presentiments. Amidst the trials which the girl had experienced at Lourdes since the age of ten, when ruin had compelled her family to leave the Boly mill, and then subsequently at Bartrès, when she felt more unwell and less well treated, she had been aware of an inward conviction that Jesus in the Blessed Sacrament would be her consoler. Pure and loyal souls are supernaturally guided by the Holy Spirit.

Her foster-mother had promised to send her to the catechism class, but she did nothing of the kind. To make up for that, she made an attempt to teach Bernadette in the evening, but not having attended school the girl's memory was bad and she was ignorant of French. If the elements of Christian doctrine had been explained to her in the patois, as M. Barbet, the Bartrès schoolmaster did once or twice, she might have shown an unexpected understanding of religious matters ; but Madame Aravant contented herself with reading the letter of the catechism to her and making her repeat it. Bernadette understood nothing of it and the farmer's wife would throw aside the book, saying : ' Go along with you ! You are only a little dunce and you will never know anything ! '

Then it was that, as her godmother, Bernarde Casterot, informs us, in the month of January 1858, whilst watching her little flock, she saw a neighbour from Lourdes passing by and told him : 'I am tired of being here. Let my parents know that I want to come home to Lourdes, to go to school and prepare for my first Communion. Tell them to come for me.' The parents did not come, and Bernadette then asked the farmer Aravant to let her go to Lourdes. She remained a few days, came back and told them : 'I must return home. M. le Curé is going to prepare the children for their first Communion, and if I go to Lourdes I shall make mine.' In fact, she left rather suddenly the following day.

Back at the Rue des Petits-Fossés, at the *cachot*, she resumed her place and her duties as elder sister. We shall always notice in Bernadette a tendency to give advice, and lay down the law, although it is a decreasing tendency. At fourteen, she showed a slight inclination to 'preach'; she held forth to her sister, Toinette, and her brothers, and corrected them for their slightest faults. It is from Toinette herself, her younger sister, that we learn this, and she adds this particular detail : 'She did not like me to leave my little brother to go wandering about, and that used to make me rather impatient with her; nevertheless I loved her dearly and my brothers were fonder of her than they were of me.' When asked in 1879 : 'Do you remember having sometimes reprimanded or scolded your brothers and sister before the apparitions?' Bernadette replied :

'When I saw them doing anything wrong, I scolded them.'

'Were you ever struck by your sister ?'

'I had some disputes with my sister, for neither she nor I would give in.'

At the time of the first apparitions, all the accounts make mention of the almost excessive modesty of Bernadette. Her sister, Toinette, and her friend,

Jeanne Abadie, who had just removed their clogs and did not wear stockings, were crossing the mill stream to return to the cave, when Bernadette called to them : ' Let down your skirts.' She asked Jeanne Abadie to take her on her back to carry her over, but the latter called back : ' *Pét de periclé !* If you want to cross, cross ; if not, stay where you are.' Bernadette told her not to swear. ' *Pét de periclé*,' as Toinette explains, ' is not a serious oath. It means " Thunder ! " ' Nevertheless, Bernadette told Jeanne that if she were beginning to use bad language she would never again make a companion of her. ' If you want to swear, you can go elsewhere.'

After the apparitions, the two girls began to dance in the cave. Some men working on the other side of the Gave, in the Ribère field, noticed them. Bernadette reproved them for thus making an exhibition of themselves.

These few details enable us to see the general trend of Bernadette's mind. She was extremely careful as to fitting behaviour.

This, which was her ordinary attitude, was all the more surprising in that Bernadette did not look more than ten, but she was undoubtedly pious. We know that she wore the scapular, from a priest who asked her. Later on, when asked, ' Did you say the rosary when in the fields at Bartrès ? ' she replied, ' I don't know.' She did not remember having said it, but there can be no doubt that she was in the habit of so doing. It was almost her only devotion and when struck with fear at the first apparition, her first impulse was to take from her pocket the rosary which she always carried. Toinette saw her kneeling on the ground praying and, not at all surprised, she said to Jeanne Abadie : ' Look at Bernadette praying down there ! ' Jeanne retorted : ' Pious thing ! Leave

her there. All she can do is pray ! ' Hence we
cannot doubt that a month previously at Bartrès,
when she was weary of watching her flock, she said
her rosary. She sought strength from above and
without being aware of it, although she had not the
training of Teresa Martin, she also entered into real
mental prayer.

Such was the little girl whom our Lady had
chosen to be her interpreter to men. Extremely
innocent, she does not seem to have known the
shadow of evil. Very poor, of feeble health, as her
godmother tells us, she suffered from palpitations of
the heart in addition to her asthma, when the stifling
attacks came on. She was completely ignorant and
did not even know French. She had already experienced many a trial ; she had suffered for her
parents ; for her father who, with harshness and
injustice, had been imprisoned for a week, until the
authorities had been forced to release him. We see
her evidently destined to a life of suffering. She will
be a victim, but her upbringing has already developed her natural virtues. Before all, she will do
the will of God. She will obey her parents ; she
will be very brave, and will allow nobody to influence
her when duty shows her how she should behave.
Doubtless, she has some failings, which we shall
presently discover, but her efforts, the special graces
which she will soon receive, the discipline of religious
life, will enable her to correct herself of these, and
she will become a saint—a great saint !

CHAPTER II

Bernadette During the Apparitions

The Virtue and Gift of Fortitude

WHEN the series of apparitions closed, Bernadette had received extraordinary graces which would completely transform her and exercise a decisive influence upon her supernatural destiny. During those eighteen apparitions, she would be obliged to practise virtues even to the point of heroism, and that constantly and from many points of view.

To enumerate all the virtues and gifts which Bernadette received and put into practice would be difficult and, no doubt, impossible ; we shall confine ourselves to distinguishing four of the chief. In her case, what first strikes the psychologist who studies the story of the apparitions closely is the virtue and gift of fortitude. What strikes us no less, and, perhaps, astonishes us still more, is the disinterestedness of this child, so poor, who notwithstanding so many temptations refuses categorically all the highly advantageous, and even most legitimate offers made her. An author who is familiarized with the difficulties of the spiritual life will, undoubtedly, be yet more surprised not to find in Bernadette the slightest movement of vanity, boasting, of that self-love which, according to a well-known saying, dies only a quarter of an hour after ourselves, on account of the visions that brought her an extraordinary notoriety from day to day. Finally, although it may be more hidden and difficult to penetrate than the foregoing, after Bernadette had been favoured with eighteen apparitions and with the conversation of Mary Immaculate, there was certainly in her a gift of piety that would continue to increase but which none the less existed in a developed form from that period.

We have already pointed out in preceding studies [1] that the supernatural virtues and gifts always imply the contrary or complementary qualities. As far as possible, we must endeavour to rediscover or emphasize these qualities when analysing the strength, the detachment from earthly goods, the indifference to ' celebrity ' and the piety which marked Bernadette.

Under what circumstances, above all during the apparitions, she practised the virtue and gift of fortitude no reader is unaware. Let us note, first of all, that the natural virtue of fortitude does not exist without a certain movement of the passions. The man who struggles, the fighter, is willingly carried away, whilst yet remaining master of himself. According to St. Thomas, this outburst of controlled passion is the sign of a strong will. Even though in the exercise of the wholly supernatural gift of fortitude, we find cases when saints act vehemently and with violent zeal, it remains none the less true that the supernatural character of the strength is much more striking when it is accompanied by an imperturbable *sang-froid* and an unalterable gentleness. We shall find this in the case of Bernadette.

All the accounts are at one in recognizing that during the period of the apparitions Bernadette exhibited the gift of fortitude, especially in her encounters with the Public Prosecutor, the Superintendent of Police, the local magistrate and the

---

[1] The allusion is doubtless to the author's similar study of St. Teresa of Lisieux. (Tr.)

constables. On Sunday, February 21, after the sixth vision, the civil authorities, having agreed to take action, resolved to summon Bernadette to appear before them, and by persuasions and intimidation to prevent her from returning to the grotto. When Bernadette, who looked like a frail little girl of eleven, made her appearance, M. Dutour, the Public Prosecutor, was at once impressed by her attitude. She was full of confidence yet modest, gentle and quite devoid of arrogance. ' When she appeared,' he writes, ' her countenance was calm, confident, equally free from fear or insolence. What she heard did not seem to disturb her, and what she said was uttered simply and without embarrassment.' This bearing, very simple but in reality composed of two contrary elements—on the one hand an imperturbable assurance and on the other a patient humility— is already characteristic of the supernatural Christian virtue. As St. Thomas so well explains, the qualities which are not only natural but wholly supernaturalized by grace never carry with them the corresponding defects. This virtue of fortitude, enriched with all the complementary qualities of constancy, *sangfroid*, imperturbable confidence, patience and lucid serenity, will be still more in evidence when Bernadette faces the Superintendent of Police.

M. Jacomet was a first-rate police officer. He rose rapidly and ended his career in Paris. A tall, fine, manly figure, he knew how to overawe others and, when he wished, gain their confidence. He was a ready public speaker, which rendered him formidable even to the barristers. He was observant and his penetrating glance could detect the slightest subterfuges by reading the countenances of the speakers. ' As a police officer,' writes one of his most familiar friends, ' no one knew better than he how to unmask a rogue and make him confess his guilt.' It has been said also that he ' put Bernadette through it' according to all the rules of his art. When the congregation came out from Vespers, he made the constable, Pierre Callet, point out Bernadette. Then he came forward, put his hand on her shoulder and said : 'You must come along with me.' Surprisingly calm and self-possessed, she replied : ' Yes, sir ; where you like,' and followed the Superintendent, escorted by the constable. The onlookers were saying, ' Poor Bernadette ! they are going to put you in prison,' but she answered, smiling, ' I am not afraid. If they put me there, they will soon take me out again.' Any other little girl under such circumstances would have been upset and begun to cry. Later on, her cousin, Jeanne Védère, told her that she intended to go to the grotto when access to it was forbidden. ' Don't go,' said Bernadette, ' the grotto is barricaded off, entrance is forbidden, and if the Superintendent, or those employed to watch it, saw you you would be arrested, and you would die. You are too frightened.' At this date, Jeanne Védère was over twenty years of age. Bernadette knew how afraid girls were of being taken up, sent to gaol ; the very thought of it was enough to send them distracted. A woman of Lourdes howled when cited before the court at Pau and, on her own showing, was terrified when she saw the police behind her. ' I imagined they were going to take us to prison ! ' At the thought of it alone, she lost her head. With still greater reason, the girls of the simple folk at Lourdes shared this dread.

The more we consider this question, the more astounded we are at Bernadette's coolness and composure. When the Superintendent made her enter his office, he began by questioning her with assumed good-nature and sympathy. ' Bernadette,' writes M. Estrade, who was present at the examination, ' remained seated in a perfectly natural attitude, her hands folded on her lap and her head slightly bent. Her face showed great seriousness and great simplicity.' When the Superintendent had taken down her name and age, and had made her give an account of the apparitions, ' he took his page of notes and began to cross-question the visionary, trying to entrap her into contradicting herself.' All the witnesses agree in acknowledging that when made to relate the story of the visions Bernadette was rather taciturn, answered the questions put to her very shortly, and disconcerted her visitors by her lack of imagination and of aptitude for conversation. The expression of her face seemed dull, to some she seemed insignificant ; but if anyone expressed doubts concerning the possibility of the apparitions, or of her sincerity, forthwith she was transformed, her eyes shone and her retorts could be devastating. ' If anyone tried to oppose Bernadette,' writes Fr. Duboé, who long knew her intimately at Lourdes and was the first to write her story ; ' if they pronounced her statements to be impossible, then it was her chance to triumph. An astonishing change took place in that child. Contradiction rendered her interesting. She astounded and put to silence the well-informed men who fought against her, with all their advantages of easy speech and experience, just by the sallies of her common sense and wit. At ceremonious meetings, there were some who clapped their hands at her unexpected and decisive retorts.' [1]

Accustomed as he was to battles of words, the Superintendent was to experience the sudden metamorphosis of the little peasant. In his notes, he had

[1] PP. Sempé et Duboé, *Notre Dame de Lourdes*, p. 182.

2

purposely made alterations in Bernadette's account. He had written that the Lady was nineteen years old, wore a blue dress and a white girdle. With an assurance equally tranquil and imperturbable, Bernadette replied : ' On the contrary, sir, you must put a white dress and a blue girdle. I did not say nineteen, but sixteen or seventeen. I did not say her hair hung down behind. You did not understand. It was the veil that hung down behind.'

It was in vain that he insisted. Bernadette only persisted in her previous statements, more firmly and serenely. M. Jacomet, on the contrary, began to grow annoyed. ' Bernadette,' writes J.-B. Estrade, ' corrected, without insolence but also without timidity, all the variants which he had purposely introduced into his report.' After the former, fatherly conversation, it was a veritable duel that took place, and one in which all the feints of the policeman were immediately parried, and accompanied by replies which, however innocent they might be, did not fail to wound his self-importance. Judging that he stood to gain nothing on the ground he had taken up, M. Jacomet changed his tactics.

' Becoming grave,' M. Estrade tells us, ' and looking fixedly at the child, in a slightly ironical tone, he said : " My dear Bernadette, I must tell you that I already know the story of your pretended visions. This tale is a pure invention and I know who has taught it to you." At these words, Bernadette raised her great, shining, soft, black eyes to the Superintendent—those eyes her contemporaries admired—and looking at him, said : " Sir, I do not understand you." '

Beaten again, and compelled to lower his own eyes, M. Jacomet resolved to play his last card. Suddenly showing great anger, he declared : ' I do not demand a confession, but I require of you a simple promise. Will you assure me that you will not return to the cave ? '

' Sir,' replied Bernadette, ' I do not promise you. I told the Lady that I would return there.'

' Oh, indeed ! ' cried the Superintendent, rising to his feet, ' so you think that we shall still be in the humour to listen to your fairy tales ? '

Subsequently Bernadette asserted that, before getting up, he was so furious and so flustered that, when he was trying to take some ink, he could not manage to find the hole in the inkstand. Obviously, the girl had retained all her coolness and presence of mind. The Superintendent felt that he was virtually powerless and defeated.

Forgetting himself, he grossly insulted Bernadette, and concluded his diatribe by declaring : ' Unless, this instant, you give an undertaking not to go to Massabieille again, I shall send for the constable and have you put in prison ! ' It was the last blow, and apparently the most intimidating that he attempted. Rightly deciding that all discussion was henceforth useless, Bernadette remained perfectly impassive.

Estrade, moved himself, approached the visionary and advised her kindly : ' Don't be obstinate. Consent to what M. Jacomet asks.'

' Bernadette,' as he very rightly remarks, ' understood by instinct that I had no authority to intervene in the discussion, and did not answer.'

The more we study Bernadette's attitude under this cross-examination, the more we shall admire her gift of fortitude. In all due proportion, the little girl had the same gift as that of the martyrs who appeared before the courts. She felt she had the light and the truth ; she was not afraid of police nor of prison. We may affirm without hesitation that she would not have denied the truth of the apparitions and the Lady even had she been threatened with worse sufferings.   Her assured confidence and calmness in face of the Superintendent's insults and anger are a pledge of that.

Another particular characteristic which proves Bernadette's gift of fortitude to have been really inspired and supernatural is that, however strong it might be, it never in her case carries with it, as happens only too frequently, a want of discipline and obedience to lawful authority.   Those who are strong and energetic only by nature too often end by laughing at laws, and transgressing the prohibitions of constituted authorities.   In Bernadette's case, on the contrary, we observe an unfailing obedience to her parents and her confessor, and this although there is question of a pious mission that can in no way seem reprehensible.   This prompt and almost scrupulous obedience is, let us say it again, one of the surest and most striking signs of her supernatural inspiration.

From the day of the third apparition, when the Lady so courteously asks her : ' Will you do me the pleasure of coming here during a fortnight ? ' she replies : ' Yes, if my parents allow me.'   She does in fact obtain this permission, and presents herself at the grotto on the Friday, Saturday and Sunday.   On the last-named day, when she has undergone the questioning of the Public Prosecutor and the Police Superintendent, her frightened parents forbid her to return to Massabieille.   She obeys. On Monday morning, February 22, she goes straight to school, turning neither to right nor left.   When the day is half over, after the midday meal, she again returns to the convent of the Sisters of Nevers, where she is a pupil.   Only at the moment of crossing the threshold of the main entrance does she feel herself as though drawn by a force more potent than her will, and takes the road to the grotto by going round the castle. Two constables, having noticed her from the barracks near the convent, set off on her track and soon come up with her. As though possessed by the divine inspiration that is drawing her, far from being afraid of them, Bernadette does not even seem to notice them. Those who have been on the watch since the morning, awaiting the visionary, cry out, on seeing her arrive: 'It is she! It is she!' 'It was indeed Bernadette,' says Mlle. Estrade; ' between the two policemen, she retained her simple, modest bearing. She seemed as unconcerned as though she were between her father and mother.' Another witness states: ' Nothing struck me more than to see the little girl, flanked by two stalwart constables, advance, as resolute as she was quiet, towards the grotto. When these two had asked her in a commanding tone where she was going, she had answered coldly, without either slackening her pace or turning her head: "I am going to the grotto."'

We have related elsewhere how on that day Bernadette was not gratified with the vision. The priests appointed by the Bishop to examine her wondered whether there might not have been some formal disobedience to paternal authority in her conduct, but it is clear that she was moved by a divine impulse; she could scarcely have resisted, any more than can a tree carried away by a flood. Subsequently, Bernadette explained to her cousin, Jeanne Védère, the overmastering strength of this supernatural impulse. On Wednesday, March 3, not having seen the daily vision earlier, she felt urged to return towards the end of the forenoon. Her cousin asked her whether, when she had returned thus to the cave, it had been because the Lady had been to her home to take her. Bernadette burst out laughing heartily. 'No,' she replied, 'it is a longing that I feel to see the Lady. It is so strong that nothing could stop me if I did not fear to disobey my parents.' This answer is valuable. It reveals to us both the strength from on high that nothing can resist and, at the same time, the high sense of obedience which Bernadette bore towards her parents.

On Monday, February 22, when, notwithstanding all her good will, Bernadette could not see the vision, she withdrew, deeply disappointed and quite overcome, to the Savy mill, close by, where they made her sit down to rest. She was sobbing. 'I do not know,' she said, ' how I have offended the Lady.' In reality, there was a twofold lesson contained in our Lady's absence. The Blessed Virgin willed to emphasize the obedience due in the first place, under such circumstances, to the parents; but also, and still more, to give the parents a lesson by blaming them for having so easily submitted, not to a legitimate order, which the Superintendent had no power to give them, but to his simple threat and desire. Moreover, Bernadette's mother fully grasped the sense of this lesson that came to her from on high. 'She was seated beside her child,' Mlle. Estrade tells us, ' streaming with perspiration and very pale; and from time to time cast glances of anguish at her daughter.' When questioned by Mlle. Estrade, she answered: ' The little one does not tell lies; she is not ordinarily disobedient. I had forbidden her to come to the cave, but she came all the same. She tells me she felt compelled to come by something she did not explain.' Mlle. Estrade asked the mother what she intended to do thenceforth with respect to the visits promised by her daughter to the Lady.

The mother replied: 'After what has happened to-day, I don't dare to oppose them any more.'

Throughout this episode, we see an extraordinary gift of supernatural strength united to a constant care for discipline and obedience. That same day, Bernadette had to obtain from her parents the authorization which the supernatural force had respected as far as possible, but she had also to ask advice from her confessor, the Abbé Pomian, chaplain of the hospice kept by the Sisters of Nevers. He testifies that, when asked by Bernadette, he had then replied: 'You may go. They have no right to hinder you.' Hence, this inspiration which overpowered Bernadette at the same time counselled her to submit herself to all legitimate authority. There is no question here of that strength which overrides and slights authority. Christian fortitude is never more powerful than when it is docile and patient and, notwithstanding all apparently insurmountable obstacles, attains its ends.

We might cite many striking instances of how Bernadette showed herself very serene and very energetic. During the many examinations she had to undergo by highly placed officials and the Bishop, she never failed in perfect humility, yet nevertheless she showed very firm assurance. Notably when she was made to appear at the grotto before the clergy forming the commission set up by the Bishop, and numerous witnesses, the official report cannot but testify to the perfection of her behaviour. 'She presented herself,' we read, 'with respectful humility and yet with extreme assurance. She found herself amidst this great assembly, in presence of distinguished priests whom she had never seen, but of whose mission she was aware, as calmly, and as much at her ease as though she had been alone or with her playmates.'

We do not wish to dilate unduly upon this gift of

fortitude, which is incontestable and uncontested.
We shall give one more example in Bernadette's case.
On Sunday, February 28, a week after the examinations we have related by the Public Prosecutor and
the Police Superintendent, which were ineffective,
these representatives of public authority arranged
with the local magistrate that he should summon
Bernadette to appear before him. This enquiry
before M. Rives, with the Superintendent of Police
also present, was more important and still more
intimidating than those of the previous Sunday.
Had not the magistrate sufficient authority to send
Bernadette to prison, and was he not prepared to
do so ?   Moreover, in this case the Superintendent
was acting on the instructions of the Public Prosecutor.   After High Mass, M. Jacomet, having
arranged with the district road surveyor, Léon
Latapie, to accompany him, said to the latter, as the
schoolgirls emerged from church in charge of the
Sisters : ' Go and fetch me Bernadette.' The surveyor obeyed and came to take her by the arm.   He
tells us himself that the Sisters began to cry.   Bernadette, on the contrary, after the experiences of the
last Sunday, felt more sure of herself than ever.
' What do you want with me ? ' she asked.   ' I
answered, " Little one, you must come with us." '
She began to laugh and said, ' Hold me tight, or I
shall run away ! '   She was taken to M. Rives, the
magistrate.   He addressed the child in patois, without
showing her the slightest consideration.   ' So you're
there, you gadabout ? ' he asked.   ' Yes, sir.   I'm
here,' she replied.   ' Why are you making so many
people run after you like this ?   We are going to put
you in prison.'   ' I am ready,' was the answer.   ' Put
me there, but see that it is strong and firmly shut, or
I shall escape.'   ' I will make you die in prison.'

' I am not going to give up going. Next Thursday is the last day.'

At that moment, the Sister Superior of the hospice entered and, in tears, besought them: ' Gentlemen, I beg of you, leave the child to us. Don't kill her!' Bernadette remained impassive and calm. Her confidence, tinged with gallantry, and recalling the last days of Joan of Arc, did not amount to insolence. She withdrew without having renounced her pious mission. ' Bernadette must have been a saint,' cried Latapie, ' and powerfully inspired to have shown such coolness as she did.'

Later on, after the celebrated fortnight of successive apparitions, when the grotto was barricaded and the public forbidden to approach it, unlike others who acted otherwise, Bernadette made no attempt to infringe the legal prohibition. She respected it and made her friends do likewise. When the widow of Admiral Bruat, with her three daughters and a religious, came to pray at Lourdes, she had Bernadette presented to her. The religious, Sister Antoine, of the Bon Secours, asked the girl to accompany them to the grotto. What more tempting invitation! Bernadette might have disdained the police authority, she was assured of impunity, and yet she firmly refused. ' No,' she said, ' I have been forbidden; I cannot.' She led the visitors only as far as the bridge. Père Cros, having asked for an exact account from Bernadette's cousin, who had become a Cistercian and was undoubtedly the person to whom the visionary spoke most confidentially, Jeanne Védère answered, among other matters: ' Since I disapproved of the conduct of the Superintendent, Bernadette said to me: " We must not stop at the men; it is God who is allowing it. We must be patient." She was always resigned,' she added; always she saw God's command or His permission.   When she heard anyone speaking against those gentlemen on account of what they had done, with respect to the grotto, she skilfully tried to change the conversation.   When she did not succeed, she made excuses for them.

'" Pray," she would say, showing me a statue of our Lady that was in her room, " and have patience. We must not stop at the men." '   This essentially Catholic line of conduct, which recalls the attitude of the early Christians, seems to us to constitute a more certain proof of Bernadette's supernatural inspiration and of her vocation to sanctity than passing instances of heroism, doubtless admirable but not exceeding the limits of natural qualities.

During the retreat preparatory to her first Communion, a strange lady, who was talking to Bernadette, asked her: ' If M. le Curé were to forbid you to go to the grotto and the Blessed Virgin were to order you to go, what would you do ? '   Bernadette replied, without either embarrassment or hesitation: ' I would come and ask permission from M. le Curé.'

When we recognize in the girl this resolute attitude to obey before all else, even though she might hear the Lady order her to go to the grotto, we cannot doubt that the indomitable strength that animated her, united to an interior sense of submission towards lawful authority, despite all else, was inspired of God. In Bernadette, the virtue and gift of fortitude, when analysed psychologically and with the aid of fixed theological principles, stand revealed as evidently Christian, transcendent, inspired, supernatural.

CHAPTER III

BERNADETTE DURING AND AFTER THE APPARITIONS

Her Disinterestedness, Humility and Piety

AFTER the virtue and gift of fortitude, what impresses the reader in Bernadette and her family is undoubtedly their absolute and unfailing disinterestedness as regards the goods of this world, from the moment that her supernatural mission is in question.

François Subirous and his wife were the poorest inhabitants of Lourdes. The parents were day labourers. In order to earn a few coppers, the mother often went out in the morning to look for a log in the forest of Batsurguère and came to sell it in the Place du Marcadal. The children went about the streets provided with a basket, picking up rags and bones which they sold in order to buy bread. The father had been unjustly accused of having stolen some flour from Maisongrosse, the baker. It had been alleged against him as a crime that, before daybreak, he had picked up a plank that had been left at the municipal offices and which no one had ever come to claim. When the first visions took place, M. Dutour, the Public Prosecutor, suspected the family of fraudulent dealing. At the time of the second vision, Bernadette was taken in and kindly treated by Mme. Millet. The magistrate sought grounds of accusation in this hospitality, but he frankly admitted that it had been freely offered. M. Jacomet, the Police Superintendent, was persuaded from the first that Bernadette's visions masked some self-interested trickery.

The two men agreed in keeping the humble dwelling of the Subirous under observation. M. Estrade writes that underlings used to come in the evening and listen through the house door, in order to catch the inmates by surprise when they were talking over the supposed fraudulent scheme. On pretext of helping them, pretended friends presented themselves at the same dwelling to make compromising offers of money. ' These spies,' he writes, ' kept harking back everywhere to the unfortunate affair of the theft, and left it to be understood that there was question of some hidden and similar misconduct.'

These incidents help us to understand the almost forced disinterestedness which led the Subirous not to accept anything that might have the least appearance of reward whenever the visions or the mission of Bernadette were concerned, whether directly or indirectly.

So numerous are the proofs of this disinterestedness, that to cite them all is impossible. From the time of the first examination by the Public Prosecutor, Bernadette answered: ' We do not receive anything from anybody.' Nevertheless, the gossip went round Lourdes that the family received gifts secretly. André Sajoux, who owned the Subirous' home in the Rue des Petits-Fossés, and who himself lived on the first floor, declared as regards this subject: ' If Bernadette had not forbidden me to accept anything, I should be one of the richest men in Lourdes. I have been offered a great deal. Once some gentlemen coming from Pau offered me handfuls of gold pieces. There were three of them, and they arrived at our house about two o'clock in the morning. They brought a girl, already fairly big, who had long been ill. They begged Bernadette to embrace her and touch her chest. Annoyed, Bernadette said to them: "I do not undertake to cure people. Wash her with water from the spring." When they left, I went with them to the door, and it was there that they offered me a lot of money. I took nothing.'

During the two years following the apparitions, Bernadette lived with her family. She attended the school kept by the Sisters, but was very often kept away by the sick or pilgrims who came to visit her. Some months after the last vision, her parents rented a humble lodging near the church, and were subsequently settled in a poor mill let to them. There at every moment people came asking for Bernadette, when they did not go to seek her at the Sisters' convent. If the girl had only consented to accept the gifts in money and in kind that were left secretly, unknown to her parents, she need not have waited long before being amply provided for.

Doctor Dozous, who bore witness to her fierce determination in defeating all such attempts, could not refrain from rendering moving homage to Bernadette's detachment. ' Humble, modest child,' he writes, ' detached from earthly goods, allow a man who had the happy privilege of caring for your health to speak of your poverty. By opening your hands to the riches men would have poured into them, you might have become rich. You are poor, and you would not depart from that poverty by accepting the gifts of every kind which the good people drawn to the scene of your prayers vied with one another in offering you!' [1]

The following incident is that most frequently cited by the biographers as an example of this scrupulous detachment: Bernadette's little brother,

[1] *La Grotte de Lourdes*, p. 83.

Pierre-Bernard, who was also her godson, had accepted two francs from a lady for having taken her bottle to the spring and filled it. When, overjoyed, he returned home, bringing the two francs to his elder sister, she promptly gave him a sharp box on the ear and made him take back the money at once to the lady. When he returned, she searched all his pockets and strictly forbade him ever again to accept anything. Subsequently, Pierre-Bernard told one of the Sisters of Nevers that it had been the sharpest slap he had ever received in his life ! When it was a matter of accepting proffered gifts, she carried her scruple still further. One evening a lady brought some oranges. Bernadette declined them but consented, however, to take them on condition that the donor ate them with the family. One day, someone secretly slipped some gold coins into her apron pocket. As soon as she noticed them, she rejected them as though the gold had burnt her. She would not even accept pious objects, such as rosaries or medals. Mgr. Thibault, Bishop of Montpellier, when returning from Cauterets, stayed with the parish priest of Lourdes. He offered Bernadette a valuable gold-mounted coral rosary, indulgenced by Pius IX. One of the priests who accompanied him said: ' The very sight of this precious object could not have failed to leave any of us impressed.' To the Bishop's pressing and gracious offers, Bernadette would only reply simply : ' Thank you, but I have one.'

Similarly there were many attempts made to secure the rosary which she had used during the apparitions. A near relative of the Pope was insistent in his efforts to gain possession of it. Bernadette remained adamant in her refusal. Another prelate, after having argued with Bernadette for a long time, concluded by

saying: ' Yes, indeed, you have beheld the Immaculate Virgin. Let me see your rosary.' Bernadette
showed it to him, and he said to her: ' My child,
you must give it to me.' ' Oh no! Father.' He
insisted so much that Bernadette handed it to him.
He took it, clasped it in his hands and kissed it
reverently. To show his gratitude, he offered her
another rosary of considerable value.[1] The beads
were white on a gold chain. On seeing it, the child
exclaimed: ' Father, keep your rosary. It would be
unsuitable for me. No, thank you.' Again he
urged her, and added: ' Let me see your scapular.'
She pulled out one edge of the scapular. ' You
must give it to me.' ' No, Father; I cannot give it
to you.' ' Your scapular is big enough to divide.
Give me half of it.' Bernadette refused. M.
Peyramale, who witnessed the scene, begged him not
to importune her further, saying: ' Bernadette knows
why she cannot give away either her rosary or her
scapular.' Finally, offering her a considerable sum
of money, the prelate said: ' My child, I know that
your parents are poor. Take it for them.' ' No,
thank you,' replied Bernadette. ' My parents can
work.'

With more simplicity, the good peasants coming
in from the country brought baskets filled with
poultry, butter, eggs, cheeses, fruits and vegetables.
The Fathers of Bétharram, who relate the fact, were
very surprised to see them return with their provisions.
Here is a special case, when seemingly Bernadette
and the Subirous family might have accepted what

[1] As here expressed, the account may suggest that the priest retained the rosary. This, however, was not the case, as is clear from
the subsequent remark of M. Peyramale and from the Saint's emphatic
statement later on. She permitted the pilgrim only to handle it. She
had reason to believe that it was actually stolen from her. See p. 44.
(Tr.)

was offered them. A wealthy family, on the way to Cauterets, wished to see Bernadette. They offered the child a sum of money which she declined. They requested M. Peyramale to intervene, and consigned the money to him to be expended for the benefit of the Subirous family. The priest requested the baker, Maisongrosse, to supply them with bread free of charge. A twelve pound loaf was offered them, but the family refused it and the baker returned the money to the Curé. Bernadette's parents refused gifts from everybody, no matter whom.

After Vespers in the convent chapel, a wealthy lady had Bernadette presented to her. She urged her to accept money. She had been recommended by the Curé. Bernadette refused imperturbably. M. Peyramale, who had been immediately informed of the incident, wrote to the Bishop: ' In the moral order, it is the most remarkable phenomenon to see how this child of the people refuses the offers made her, and that in so dignified a manner.'

M. Azun de Bernétas, having written a small work on the apparitions, offered Bernadette a copy. With a quick gesture, the girl withdrew her hand, and thanked him with an expression on her face as decided as it was modest. The author himself tells how he turned to her mother, saying: ' By accepting this book you will share in fifty-two Masses daily. To decline this benefit, which is purely spiritual, would not be edifying.' ' If it is only a spiritual benefit,' said the mother to her daughter, ' you may take it.' Then, out of obedience, Bernadette took the book.

Whatever may be said about it, let us take note that this disinterested behaviour on the part of the Subirous family, and of Bernadette in particular, was not carried to the point of contempt. It happens frequently enough that the poor hate the homes, the manners, and all the comforts enjoyed by well-to-do persons, but such hatred is entirely natural. Strictly speaking, it is merely a reversed love of these good things; a longing which they are powerless to gratify and which has turned to bitterness. Such was not at all Bernadette's attitude. By a favour, or a grace that was wholly supernatural; having, moreover, gained experience of heavenly and infinite good things through her visions, she soared far above the covetousness and envy of this world. At the time of the first apparitions, the Sergeant-Major of the Lourdes police sent his wife to offer some money to Bernadette's parents, in order to make her speak. ' She looked at the money,' he tells us, ' without showing either contempt or revulsion, but she did not take it.' This life-like, and very precise, remark gives us a perfectly correct idea of the detachment and the virtue of poverty as found in Bernadette. Even as a religious, she will never feel any bitter zeal regarding the wealth possessed by those who pass for the happy folk of this world. She will not even know that sort of irritation experienced by certain religious reformers, and especially by their disciples, when seeing the expenditure and abuse of riches. She will remain in peace, with her mind above it all, knowing that the happiness promised her by our Lady is to be derived from heavenly treasure. Had not the incomparable joys she had experienced been caused by the vision of Mary Immaculate ? That was why she had said herself and had taught her brothers to say: ' I want nothing, sir.'

One witness has said, and for us the words sum up the whole matter: ' Bernadette looked for nothing from this world.'

Another gift, as we have said, still more astonishing than her detachment from earthly goods, and of which the source was clearly a divine grace due to the intercession of the Immaculate Virgin, was the absolute absence of vanity in this girl with respect to everything concerning the visions, and her indifference to the signs of admiration, and even veneration, that were thoughtlessly lavished upon her by those who believed in her and by pilgrims.

From the time of the first visions, the crowd gathered around the grotto in daily increasing numbers. When Bernadette arrived, they stood closer together and spontaneously made room for her. Jean-Baptiste Estrade has justly remarked that when she came to Massabieille, accompanied by her mother on February 20, after the fifth apparition, ' she was neither astonished nor moved to find the crowd awaiting her there. She advanced beneath the rock with the same air as though she had been a simple spectator, and went to kneel in her usual place. Without paying attention to the eyes fixed upon her, she took out her rosary and began to pray.' This attitude of perfect indifference to the enthusiastic expressions of approval, and sometimes to the mocking criticisms of some spectators, was so remarkable that no one failed to notice it. To tell the truth, whilst the apparitions lasted, there was no great merit on Bernadette's part for, as she said herself: ' I am so absorbed by the thought of the Lady that I see nothing.' But when she made her way through the crowd in order to reach her place near the rock, when the onlookers numbered as many as twenty thousand, as happened on March 4; when it was necessary to escort her, to force a passage for her by putting up barricades; when she had enough presence of mind to call to her cousin before surrendering herself to the ecstasy; when, owing to force of circumstances, the commissary or the soldiers placed themselves at her disposal, she might well have felt some emotions of complacency or vanity when thus made aware of the incalculable importance of the part she was playing. Yet never did our Lady allow her to be spoilt by any thought of pride.

One of the visionaries of La Salette, Maximin, does not seem to have been so completely immunized against all feelings of touchiness and self-love with respect to his vision. The incredulity of the priests pricked him to the quick, and it was just that feature which disconcerted the holy Curé of Ars, and led him to suspend his judgement. Bernadette, on the contrary (and for her the situation presented itself fairly often, when well-informed visitors multiplied captious objections) always retained her peace of soul. Having answered as satisfactorily as she could, she remained silent when faced with ill will or obstinate incredulity. She replied simply: 'I cannot explain all these things to you. I am not learned.' Or again: 'The Blessed Virgin bade me say what I have seen, but not to make you believe.'

M. Peyramale relates this incident. A priest, having heard Bernadette tell him that the apparition wore a blue girdle, quoted in opposition to her liturgical books wherein that colour is excluded from those of certain sacred vestments. Bernadette contented herself with replying: 'For my part, I know nothing about that, but I saw that her girdle was blue.' The priest continued to hold forth, mentioning other books, according to which blue might harmonize with divine worship in the representation of certain mysteries. At this point, Bernadette, whom the learned speaker was forgetting, said simply: 'Those books do not agree with the others.'

This unexpected reflection put an end to the argument.

Canon Ribes, founder of the Lourdes hospice, pointed out to Bernadette that the Blessed Virgin could not have ordered her to go to the parish priest in order to ask for a procession, since for the latter the Bishop's permission was necessary. The Canon, who relates this conversation, tells us that he was expecting this answer: ' If M. le Curé requires the Bishop's permission, he has only to ask it.' Bernadette replied much better. ' If it is impossible, Father, I was mistaken; but I heard those words as I heard the others.' Canon Ribes added: ' She spoke these words with admirable simplicity, and I was seized with such an impression of respect that I ceased my objections.' At the close of 1861, one pilgrim was granted the favour of seeing Bernadette at the hospice. ' She came in,' he says, ' in her simple peasant's dress, quite naturally, without shyness as without self-importance. I was impressed by her calmness, by the simple way she told me the story of her vision; she spoke as though they were ordinary events which had happened to a third party.' Fernand Laudet has explained this sort of indifference which rendered her, so to speak, a stranger to the events she was relating, as an acquired habit resulting from constantly repeating the same facts. It was like a lesson learnt by heart, which she repeated mechanically without being any longer impressed by the divine realities which she was relating. This explanation does not suffice, for on February 21, from the fourth day of the celebrated fortnight of successive apparitions, she was questioned by the Abbé Pène, one of the curates, who had her brought to him. She described to him the visions with which she had been favoured since February 11. ' She did so,' he writes, ' in a very calm and natural manner, without fear, without ostentation, with *indifference*, as though she were performing a duty.'

Thus, from the outset Bernadette was evidently granted the grace of a surprising simplicity with respect to the divine privileges; which astonishing indifference cannot be explained on the grounds that it had become an inveterate habit.

The Lourdes schoolmaster, M. Clarens, who questioned Bernadette all day on February 28, and believed her, was also struck by this entire absence of self-importance in her case. ' The sort of *indifference*,' he writes, ' with which she spoke, the assurance of her answers, the simplicity of her remarks, caused my first unfavourable convictions to collapse. Go and listen to her, you who pride yourselves on being strong-minded, and you will not come away without being completely disarmed.' Some months later, Bernadette was at Tarbes. A Superior of the senior seminary had her brought to him. It was market day, and the students' relatives having come to see them, the former were coming to the parlour in groups. Bernadette was very interested at seeing these young clerics, and the priest who was questioning her writes: ' She seemed more concerned with the sight she was seeing—for the first time, it is true—than with the rôle Providence had called upon her to play and the interest which the events at Lourdes, and her own person, inspired in everybody. One would have said that for her the great happening was a matter of *indifference*. This detachment, above all, strongly impressed me.'

So then, let us repeat it. It was the same indifference which we can verify in the earliest days that we find again years afterwards. It was certainly not acquired, as some would endeavour to make us believe, but was, on the contrary, a gratuitous and infused grace. In September, 1863, the sculptor, M. Fabisch, who had to produce the first statue of *Our Lady of Lourdes*, came to interview Bernadette. ' Not the greatest men of genius,' he writes, ' have ever produced anything so sweet, and at the same time so profound, as the expression of this girl; so simple, so unsophisticated, consumptive through and through, and who has apparently not the least doubt in the world that she has received an outstanding privilege.'

The outstanding privilege to which M. Fabisch is referring evidently consists in the apparitions at Massabieille, but for those who knew Bernadette this immunity from vainglory, which had been freely bestowed upon her from the beginning, was equally no mean favour. ' There was nothing about her,' attests Sister Victorine, in whose charge Bernadette had been placed, ' that betrayed the slightest shadow of preoccupation with self, curiosity or astonishment. In this respect, I have always found her faultless, thanks to a special privilege granted to her by God. I never noticed in her any sign of vanity and self-love with respect to the extraordinary graces she had received, the compliments, praise and marks of veneration that were showered upon her.' Often visitors knelt before her asking her blessing. One day she was washing her hands in the kitchen when a priest came in, followed by a lady and her children. The priest knelt and asked Bernadette to bless him. Her reply was: ' I cannot bless anyone.' He insisted. ' Say, " O Blessed Virgin, who hast appeared to me, bless this priest and his family." ' Bernadette was annoyed and embarrassed, but in order to get rid of him, and in all simplicity, she repeated those words.

One day, when Sister Victorine was going down

to the grotto with Bernadette, someone behind her
said: 'If only I could cut off a small piece of her
dress!' Bernadette, who had the ready retort and
blunt speech of the people, turned round and
exclaimed: 'What an idiot you are!'

When she was at the hospice, the throng of
pilgrims who wished to see her was so great, and
Bernadette so exhausted by the visits, that the
Sisters were compelled to set a limit to them; nevertheless, the crowd remained in the courtyard and in
the street. Then they would take Bernadette to a
window which was then opened, and she would bow
from there. The pilgrims showed their veneration
by calling her 'the Saint,' and the privileged child
of the Blessed Virgin. She was very wearied and
she detested these exhibitions. Sister Victorine tells
how one day, as she went towards the window,
Bernadette remarked: 'I am a curiosity!' We may
guess that the good religious toned down somewhat
the original expression. From the Process of Canonization, we learn that Bernadette said quite simply,
with a spice of humour: 'You are showing me off
as though I were a curious beast!'

Never did she vary in her indifference and her
boredom with respect to the ovations to which she
was obliged to submit. 'She showed herself no
more affected by the public veneration after years
had gone by than she had done at the beginning. At
the sight of some pious pictures which she was given
to autograph, and in which she was pictured, she
exclaimed in a tone of deep conviction: 'What
nonsense!'

Although this indifference to marks of honour,
this very special humility, was a divine gift, Bernadette
was careful to guard the virtue of humility very
strictly, and she could justify her behaviour with

reasons as excellent as any spiritual director could have given. The parish priest and Vicar Forane of Vic wanted to know whether Bernadette was at all vain of her visions, and if she showed any self-love in making others believe in them.

' Is it true,' he asked her, ' that you have seen the Blessed Virgin ? '

' Yes, Very Reverend Father.'

' For my part, I do not believe that you have seen her.'

With a sort of patient indifference, Bernadette remained silent.

' Well,' he insisted, ' have you nothing to answer ? '

' What do you want me to answer ? '

' You ought to make me believe that you have really seen our Lady.'

' Oh, she did not tell me to make you believe it.'

The priest then went on to remark that several other girls were holier than she, and more worthy of the heavenly favour. Bernadette replied : ' Oh, as for that, it is as the Blessed Virgin saw fit to do.'

' In the tone of her replies,' witnesses the Dean, ' one could detect nothing that betrayed the slightest annoyance, still less wounded self-love. The girl's face remained perfectly serene. She kept silence.' He continued :

' You must be very proud of having seen our Blessed Lady ? '

' Oh why ? ' was the reply of Bernadette, who spoke little and very much to the point.

' In your place, I should be very proud.'

' Oh,' rejoined the girl, ' she has taken me for her servant.'

The Abbé Pène, curate of Lourdes, who was present at the interview, was secretly enjoying, not without a spice of mischief, the Dean's embarrassment.

He tells us expressly that the latter was nonplussed, and could not say another word. ' I took up the conversation myself,' he adds :

" Then you are the servant of the Blessed Virgin ? "

" Yes, Father."

" And what wages does she give you ? "

" Oh," she replied, smiling shrewdly, " we have not made the contract yet."

" But how much do you think she will give you ? "

" Oh, she will not be satisfied with me and will dismiss me." '

Bernadette knew quite well that, at Lourdes and in the neighbourhood, maids were taken for some time on trial before the contract was made and the rate of wages fixed. When employers were not satisfied, they dismissed the said maids. That was why Bernadette said, in effect: ' When she has given me a trial as a maid, our Lady will dismiss me.'

We do not share Bernadette's opinion, and history itself has decided against her. The Blessed Virgin was certainly very satisfied at seeing that the girl considered herself as an unprofitable servant. Was she not repeating in some sense, after her own fashion, *Ecce ancilla Domini !* ' Behold the handmaid of the Lord ! ' Our Lady did not dismiss her. She retained her in her service forever, and without being discouraged and, as we shall see, without ever rebelling against the difficulties, Bernadette will remain until her death a very humble and magnanimous servant of Mary.

When treating of the gifts of the Holy Ghost, in his *Summa Theologica*, St. Thomas Aquinas argues by analogy in assimilating them to the instincts and aptitudes which are innate.[1] The instincts, especially,

[1] *Summa Theol.*, I, II, Q.LXVIII, a. 2-4.

even those that are most highly developed and also, although in a lesser degree, the innate aptitudes, offer this distinctive characteristic, that they act as perfectly at the beginning as at the end. To cite familiar examples taken from nature : the bird sings and builds its nest, the bee constructs its hive and combs as perfectly the first time as they ever will do later on. Napoleon declared that at the age of twenty-six, in the war in Italy, he had been as able a general as he was in his later campaigns. The case is the same, in due proportion, with the supernatural gifts, especially when these are conferred upon very young and ignorant persons called to an extra-ordinary mission. We have tried to establish the fact that among the divine gifts freely bestowed upon Bernadette, the first place belonged to the gifts of *fortitude*, *detachment* from earthly goods, and *humility* with respect to the divine graces, and the tokens of admiration or veneration lavished upon her by the crowd in so unmeasured a fashion. From the first days of the apparitions, Bernadette shows herself, under all circumstances, as perfectly strong, as abso-lutely disinterested, as destitute of all conceit as she will be twenty years later. The case is not the same as regards what concerns the gift of piety. We shall endeavour to show that after the visions Berna-dette had been, as says Père Cros, 'trained in a won-derful school,' the school of our Blessed Lady; but this gift of piety was thenceforth like a shrub planted by God, which was to become in time a great tree.

During the two years immediately following the apparitions, Bernadette lived with her family. Her parents, as we have said, had been let a small mill below the Fort. Bernadette went to school, but was frequently absent, owing to the pilgrims who asked

for her and even went in search of her as far as the
hospice.

At first, the development in her of the gift of
piety does not seem to have made striking progress,
but when she was studied more closely it was not
long before the observer noticed exceptional signs of
a devotion that was hidden and deep.   Thus it was
that they admired her way of making the Sign of the
Cross.   There was a wealth of teaching in it and all
who saw her were edified.   Sister Victorine, who was
ordered at the hospice to watch over Bernadette
particularly, and who looked after her with motherly
care from her arrival in November 1861 until her
departure for Nevers in July 1866, says: ' As for her
piety, during several years it seemed very ordinary.
Notwithstanding, from a number of signs one could
perceive that she had received from God a special
gift of piety.   Thus, for instance, she made the Sign
of the Cross reverently, slowly, with a dignity, a
grace, not often noticed in the most devout people.
When she was alone and could not have known that
she was being watched, she made no change what-
soever in the beautiful way she made the Sign of the
Cross.'

The rosary, which she had been accustomed to
saying from early childhood, became her essential devotion, to which she remained by preference attached
from the time when she had said it at Massabieille,
in the presence of the Blessed Virgin and, we might
say, with her.   The poor beads, worth a few coppers,
which she had then held in her hands, were infinitely
precious to her and she never consented to give them
to anyone.   When her cousin, Jeanne Védère, had
asked her to touch three rosaries which she possessed,
Bernadette had retorted: ' What!   Are you like the
rest ?   And what do you want me to do for you ?

I am not a priest !' However, after a moment's thought, she added: 'Give me yours, and I will touch them with mine.' She twisted and re-twisted them into her own, and then returned them, saying: 'Keep them; not because I have touched them, but because they have touched the rosary I had during the apparitions.' Some pilgrims, and even certain visiting priests, claimed to have received that precious rosary which Bernadette had used during the visions. She declared on her deathbed: 'I never gave away that rosary I used during the apparitions. I refused to change it for a gold-mounted one which an Archbishop offered me at the Presbytery. One day, after having recited it, I put it in my pocket. In the evening I could not find it, either in my pocket or in the house, in spite of all my searching, and I was exceedingly sorry. If anyone is sure that he has it, he must have stolen it. I would never have consented to give it to anybody.' Of course, she lost no time in procuring another and saying her *Aves* thereon as devoutly as on the one that had disappeared. Sister Victorine states: 'Several times daily, she would be found saying the rosary. She was never without it, even at night, and spent her sleepless hours in reciting it.' Bernadette herself said: 'The rosary is my favourite prayer.'

In an earlier work,[1] we drew attention to the longing Bernadette had felt to make her first Communion. We have related also how she edified M. Peyramale during the retreat preparatory to that great ceremony. She retained a great devotion to the Blessed Sacrament, and that would always be one of the outstanding features of her piety. From the year following her first Communion, she communicated every fortnight. Questioned during the Process

[1] *Histoire exacte des Apparitions de Notre-Dame de Lourdes à Bernadette.*

of Canonization, a religious attested that she had
heard the following account from the lips of the
parish priest himself. Having to give Holy Communion to the children at the hospice, M. Peyramale
asked God for a sign to reassure him as to Bernadette's
divine mission. When he communicated her, he
observed a luminous halo framing her face. After her
first Communion, Bernadette always prepared carefully to receive the Eucharist, and made her thanksgiving with deep recollection. ' She greatly appreciated and loved Holy Communion,' says Sister
Victorine, ' and prepared herself for it well. Even
during her most painful attacks of illness, after
sleepless nights, she rose in order to communicate.
At night, I would give her some pastilles to stop her
cough : " No, Sister," she would say, " I should fall
asleep with a cough lozenge in my mouth and
should be unable to receive Communion." '

Most certainly, the intimate converse which
Bernadette had had with our Lady had remained
impressed upon her memory, and was for her a quite
special spiritual direction. Had our Lady revealed
to her any circumstances in detail ? It would seem
so, and when we come to consider the vocation of
her cousin, Jeanne Védère, the premature death of
another cousin and her godfather, we shall give more
decisive proofs. The prayer taught her by the
Mother of God, which she said every day, the three
secrets revealed to her during the apparitions and
which she kept jealously, never telling them to anyone
even on the day of her death, were also for her precious
rules of conduct. When someone asked her : ' Did
those secrets concern your religious vocation ? ' she
answered : ' It was a question of something more
important than that.' One priest plied her with
questions on this matter :

' Did the Blessed Virgin tell you any secrets ? '

' Yes, Father.'

' How many ? '

' Three.'

' The newspapers have said that she told you four.'

' No, she told me three only.'

' Are these secrets for you ? '

' Yes, Father.'

' Do they concern you only ? '

' Yes, Father.'

' Is there question of you alone in these secrets ? '

' Yes, Father.'

Bernadette's persistence in maintaining that the secrets concerned only her personal conduct leave us in no doubt but that they were for her and for her alone; precious and important advice which she must always bear in mind. When studying her spiritual and religious life, we must, therefore, take into account this essential part in Bernadette's spiritual direction which, from the first, our Lady reserved to herself.

We know, because the girl herself affirmed the fact later on, that she found she could nearly always recall the outward aspect of Mary Immaculate, such as she had appeared to her at Massabieille, unless, however, she had not been so good; then, despite all her efforts, she could no longer remember the heavenly portrait. As long as she lived at Lourdes, she frequently went to pray at the grotto. She has told us that her happiest days were those when the Sisters took her there. Later, as a religious at Nevers, she owned that she went daily to the grotto in spirit; there she doubtless found again the precious teaching she had received there.

The fundamental principles of Bernadette's

spirituality should not be sought elsewhere than in the well-known reminders: 'I do not promise to make you happy in this world, but in the next.' 'Penance! Penance! Penance!' 'Pray for sinners.' Bernadette will never seek to be happy in this world; she will endure physical and moral trials with heroic patience. At the end of her life, when purified from her imperfections, she will become clearly aware that her very special vocation is to be a victim of expiation. A few years after the apparitions, she will already be living by that primordial truth which we noted from the time of her sojourn at Bartrès: 'I stayed there because I thought God willed it.' To submit herself to the divine will, to preserve her patience, such will be one of the most fundamental characteristics of her conduct. 'I am as content,' she said, ' to stay in bed as I should be if I could go to the grotto. God wills it so. May His will be done! Do not pity me. When anyone does what God wills, there is no cause for pity.' This heroic submission to the divine will is to lead Bernadette very far and very high in the always arduous way of holiness.

CHAPTER IV

The Defects of Her High Qualities and how She Strove to Correct Them

THE extraordinary visions with which Bernadette had been favoured, the conversations which she had had with our Lady, the counsels she had received, even the gifts of the Holy Spirit that had been freely conferred upon her to enable her the better to carry out her providential mission, had not made her a saint. After the apparitions she would work to correct herself and to become perfect.

Among her most noteworthy defects, Sister Victorine, who had known her intimately for six years, singled out first self-opinionatedness and obstinacy. Although a child of the Pyrenees, Bernadette was as stubborn as a Breton. She became rooted in her ideas, did not give in willingly, and did not easily recognize that she had been in the wrong. The majority of the witnesses to her religious life will emphasize this natural imperfection as her dominant fault. It must be said also that it implied a fine quality: energy and consistency of the will; but this quality was carried to excess. The Sister notes how one day she persisted for a long time in wanting to go home. ' She yielded to the force of the reasons given her only after a fairly long period of sulking.' One day, probably a Monday, she took it into her head not to lay aside her Sunday dress, which among pupils in a boarding school was a sufficiently strange anomaly, and was noticed by everybody. Bernadette, who, as we have seen, was utterly indifferent to honours, to popular ovations, and who from that point of view seemed destitute of self-love, nevertheless remained a woman, and was a little bit vain as regards dress.

'One of her schoolfellows,' says the Sister, 'influenced her in this direction, and I surprised her in the act of altering a skirt in order to enlarge it and give the effect of a crinoline.' This taste for a crinoline may seem incomprehensible to us to-day,[1] but we must know that at the period this rather ridiculous fashion was a veritable craze in the feminine world. One of the eldest and most fervent among the Children of Mary preferred to leave the sodality rather than give up her crinoline. Later on, Bernadette exclaimed: 'Crinolines! They are diabolical!' She remembered how she herself had not escaped the infatuation of the moment. On another occasion, she was found inserting a piece of wood into a corset to do duty as a stay-bone. The Sister adds that this fever of feminine preoccupation with dress soon passed away from the girl, leaving no trace behind.

A more serious fault, and one which she retained almost to the eve of her death, was her quickness to react, which was carried to the point of impatience, when she was opposed or pestered. At such times her retorts were extremely prompt, to the point, and sometimes wounding. From the environment in which she had lived so long she had acquired the habit of answering back rather violently, and without toning down her language in the way a more refined upbringing would have taught her to do. We must

[1] Fr. Petitot wrote in 1935!

4

admit, moreover, that in her case it was also a matter of temperament. Sickly since childhood, she was highly strung, and the devil tempted her on this weak side. All her life she wrestled with this fault. 'Her lively temperament, like the Basque temperament,' attests Canon Perreau in the Canonization Process 'showed itself in quick outbursts and sallies.' It may be said that all her life she had to struggle against her character in this matter. 'These sharp retorts, these outbursts of impatience, these failings in self-control', must have been somewhat violent, for the chaplain, the Abbé Febvre, saw in these petulant movements 'the effect of a diabolic action which is uncommon.'

Among the dangerous tendencies of her temperament which the witnesses point out in passing, but upon which they do not dwell, was a propensity to become unduly affectionately attached to others. Although apparently reserved, her character contained secret springs of tenderness which, had they not been restrained, might have been a great danger for her had some particular occasion presented itself. Without divine grace, she would then have hardly escaped from that human attachment which St. Teresa of the Child Jesus calls 'a veritable misfortune.' 'How can a heart given over to human affection be intimately united to God? I feel that that is impossible. Our Lord knew that I was too weak, and did not expose me to that temptation. Beyond doubt, I should have been completely burnt up in the deceptive light of creatures.' Bernadette was as deeply sensitive to affection as Teresa, and might also have burnt herself in the 'deceptive light of creatures.' We shall see how our Lady and Providence preserved her.

The daughter of the Subirous was a very active

person. She herself wrote that she had an exuberant nature. If that nature had not been controlled, she would have given herself over to activities to the point of being absorbed by them, and that also might have been an obstacle, and not one of the least, to her sanctification. We began by drawing attention above to one of her outstanding defects, obstinacy, attachment to her own opinion. It is rare that this failing does not imply a secret pride. No doubt Bernadette always went to excess in accusing herself of being proud; nevertheless, this vice is one of the most common among mortal men, and none of the saints was exempt from it. Until her death, Bernadette strove against the most specious temptations to pride.

Having tried to enumerate briefly Bernadette's chief defects, we must now show how she corrected herself and was purified from them. No doubt she endeavoured to correct herself by repeated examinations of conscience, by meritorious efforts, by acknowledging her faults; but the most efficacious means whereby she was sanctified was providential, and it consisted in suffering. 'Bernadette,' wrote the Abbé Febvre, the chaplain who attended her until her death, 'was moulded by God rather than corrected by her own active co-operation; the passive virtues were abundant in her soul.' Notwithstanding her sharp speeches, it must be said that her life had been a life of patience. She was sanctified by God's gentle working; He fashioned her by means of the Cross and maintained her in the moral dispositions required by suffering. This manner of sanctification is not exceptional; on the contrary, it is perfectly normal. The teaching of St. John of the Cross, known by all directors nowadays, is that the soul cannot attain to perfection without passing through the passive purification of hard physical and moral trials. That was also Bernadette's opinion. ' Let suffering and troubles come,' she said, ' that is the best means of killing the human self in me.' She was speaking from experience, for from the first years after the apparitions she was very specially tried by painful maladies. ' We noticed,' writes Sister Victorine, ' that her fits of stubbornness, sulkiness, or any other failing were quickly followed by a sharper attack of physical suffering. Thus we never failed to say at such times, "She will soon be ill," and we were not mistaken. It seemed as though God willed to make her expiate her faults immediately.'

Let us notice carefully, for this remark has an essential importance, that Bernadette's bodily sufferings before her entrance into religion are destined principally to cleanse her personally of her own sins and imperfections. It is only later, when she will be leading a really contemplative life, among the Sisters of Nevers, that she will become aware that she is suffering chiefly as an expiatory victim for the salvation of sinners. There must be no mistake; many souls who have still grave faults, often unrecognized by themselves, and who cause those in close contact with them to suffer, are wont to think, a little prematurely and presumptuously, that they are supernaturally called to be victims for the salvation of others. They should first endeavour to correct and rid themselves of their defects. The vocation to vicarious suffering, properly so-called, is higher and rarer than is generally thought to-day.

During the two years after the visions, Bernadette lived with her family at a mill situated below the castle; subsequently, she entered the school of the

Sisters of Nevers as a boarder. Throughout this
period, which lasted eight years, from 1858 to 1866,
she was frequently very ill, and scarcely ever free
from suffering. But these sufferings had another
effect besides sanctifying her. During these years,
Bernadette was called by our Lady to exercise a real
apostolate. Mary had said to Estelle Fraquette,
the visionary of Pellevoisin, whom she miraculously
cured: ' I have chosen you. I choose the little and
the weak ones for my glory. I have chosen you to
proclaim and to spread this devotion.' [1] Bernadette
had been chosen to proclaim the glory and spread
the devotion of Our Lady of Lourdes. Every day,
pilgrims came to visit her, either at the mill or later
at the Sisters' hospice. By her patience in bearing
her sufferings, no less than by her candour, her
humility and her other virtues, she edified very many
and led them to believe in the supernatural power of
Our Lady of Lourdes.

M. Azun de Bernétas, one of the first who came
to question Bernadette at the mill, says: ' I was
edified by the poverty and cleanliness of her attire.
She wore the commonest sabots and woollen stockings,
a simple cotton dress, an apron of the same colour,
and a quite plain scarf round her neck. Her head
was covered with a cotton scarf. Everything was

[1] In 1876, Estelle Fraquette, a maid in the family of La Roche-
foucauld, at Pellevoisin, in the diocese of Bourges, claimed to have had
visions of our Lady, who, after curing her when she had been given up
by the doctors, showed her a white scapular bearing a representation of
the Sacred Heart. The vision, which was all in white, spoke of herself
as ' all-merciful ', and the whole theme was that of the Mercy of God.
The local ordinary, after enquiry, allowed the scapular and confra-
ternity of Pellevoisin, but with some details changed from those alleged
to have been revealed. In 1904, the Holy Office, whilst allowing both,
declared that this permission did not imply ' any direct or indirect
approbation of any visions, miracles and similar alleged facts, etc.'
(Tr.)

clean and very modest. Beside some poor furniture in her room a little shrine stood out, adorned with flowers, medals, pictures and other pious objects, which looked rich in comparison with everything else. In the centre of the altar was a statue of our Lady. " Bernadette goes to school to the Sisters of Nevers," her mother told me. " She is more ill than ever since the apparitions; however, she takes her share in household duties and helps me to look after her brothers and sisters [1]." ' It was in this modest room that visitors came to see Mary's privileged child and to question her. Her parents allowed all the pilgrims to enter indiscriminately. Certain persons, accompanied by some priests, came to see her in the month of August 1859, and one of the priests has left us an account of the interrogation to which he subjected her.

' When we reached the mill where Bernadette lived, we first found her mother. She understood the object of our visit and led us upstairs without asking any questions. Bernadette was in bed. A very frequent cough seemed to point to a little asthma. Here are almost exactly our questions and Bernadette's replies :

" Well, my child, so you are ill ? "

" Yes, Father."

" How long have you been ill ? "

" Since last Monday."

" From what are you suffering ? "

" I am suffering with my chest."

" We are not tiring you ? "

" Oh, no, Father.   I can speak to-day."

---

[1] Although the original French text alludes to ' sisters ' in the plural, we have found no reference elsewhere to any sisters of the Saint other than Toinette-Marie.   There were several brothers, not all of whom lived to grow up.   (Tr.)

" Do you not drink any water from the spring ? "

" Yes, Father."

" This water cures other sick people.   Why does it not cure you ? "

" Perhaps our Lady wishes me to suffer."

" Why should you need to do so rather than others ? "

" Oh, the good God knows." '

In a work on the apparitions, we have related the impressions of Mlle. Lacrampe. She was a pious woman and well-intentioned but, on her own showing, she was then a convinced unbeliever in the visions, and so remained for several years. Her confessor urged her to accept them, but she was unable to do so. Having been present at the ninth apparition, she had been scandalized by the behaviour of Bernadette.[1] It was she who at a later date voiced this reflection: ' Prejudice is a terrible thing ! ' which is truer than we might think. When visitors came in crowds to Lourdes, she kept the *Hôtel des Pyrénées*, and herself recounts her experiences and impressions.

' The strangers who came to us,' she says, ' used to question me about the facts concerning the grotto. I was very embarrassed. I did not wish to destroy the faith of others, but I could not affirm my own. Often these strangers were highly educated people; they related the wonderful happenings; I could not doubt that they spoke sincerely. It was difficult not to see miracles in certain cures that were described to me. Nearly all the lady visitors asked to see Bernadette, and good manners required me to accompany several to the Subirous mill. On these occasions many of my objections fell to the ground,

[1] The occasion upon which Bernadette washed in the muddy water and ate the grass.   (Tr.)

forced as I was to recognize the wisdom of Bernadette's answers, equally with her perfect sincerity and her absolute lack of self-interest. Nobody escaped from this influence. One day at the hotel, I heard four young men, who had come from Cauterets on horseback to amuse themselves at Lourdes, and joke among themselves on the subject of Bernadette, saying: " Let us go and see her." I told them: "Be on your guard, gentlemen; if you go there you will return in very different dispositions." They did not believe it at all and set off for the hospice. On their return, I said to them: " I have the right, gentlemen, to ask you for your impressions." " We have returned very much changed," was their reply. " It is true that we do not believe in the apparition, but we are convinced that this girl is incapable of deceit." '

From these quotations, we can see that although ill, or even because she was ill, Bernadette exercised a real apostolate at Lourdes; she was our Lady's witness. Fr. Sempé, the first to write the story of Our Lady of Lourdes, who knew Bernadette intimately, tells us quite correctly: ' Everyone wanted to know her, hear her, and make up their minds about her. Her relatives did not withhold her from the general curiosity; still less was she hidden at the hospice, and it would not have been right to have done so. The work of Our Lady of Lourdes bore a certain essential character of publicity; peasants, priests, men of the world, poor, great ladies, military men, all went asking to see Bernadette. A religious would call her for all without distinction. Bernadette was then the herald of the Blessed Virgin from morning till night, but at her own cost she set forth her praises.'

' More often than not,' attests Sister Victorine, ' she felt some repugnance to answering the questions of visitors, because of the fatigue these interviews caused her. All such fatigue affected her chest and led to sharp attacks of asthma. When taking her to the parlour, I used to see her stop near the door and cry and it was real crying ! " Courage," I would say; she would dry her tears, enter, look pleasant, and answer everything without becoming impatient at unfitting questions, or showing herself annoyed if anyone refused to believe her words.'

The simplicity and modesty which we have noticed left an impression of dignity upon visitors which was often irresistible. ' One saw Bernadette sought after by the great of the world. Admiration was lavished upon her. A thousand times her ears heard words that were bewildering for an ordinary girl. She was venerated as though she were a saint. The poor child never showed a vestige of self-complacency. This invincible modesty was, for all serious-minded persons, as manifest a prodigy as the cures of which they were told. For many, a quarter of an hour spent with Bernadette sufficed to make them believe everything.' [1]

Although they had verified a hundred times and proclaimed abroad her astounding and absolute indifference to the praises of visitors, and to the marks of veneration and the ovations of the crowd, those upon whom the responsibility had been laid for the moral training of Bernadette could not help fearing for her modesty, and they were ingenious in humiliating her in every way, in season and out of season. There we have a trial that might in the end have made Bernadette legitimately impatient, but her gentleness was unalterable. Among all, the Superior at the Lourdes hospice [2] distinguished

---

[1] PP. Sempé et Duboé, *Notre Dame de Lourdes*, p. 185.
[2] Mère Alexandrine Roques.

herself by her anxiety to humble the girl in public.   No doubt she did so from a sense of duty, but this spiritual pretext even if legitimate was, as happens all too frequently, an edifying outward etiquette which veiled a slight natural antipathy.   We are here confronted with a situation which we shall notice again in the life of Bernadette, and which was one of her most intimately personal and most cruel trials. There were in her, so to speak, two persons which could be distinguished.   There was the celebrated seer of the visions of Our Lady of Lourdes, enjoying an universal notoriety.   From this point of view she was valuable to a religious congregation and sought after.   They made every effort to gain possession of her and to keep her.   But there was also Bernadette, a poor little girl, ignorant, with, as we know, her not infrequent fits of the sulks, her acts of mischief, her obstinacy.   In school, although sixteen, she was not as advanced as clever children of nine, who heard her repeat her lessons.   The Sisters, who saw her from morning till night, who made her work in the kitchen and ordered her about; who spoke to her as to a very poor little girl of the people and heard her replies, ended by forgetting the seer of visions and considered her more practically only as a very ordinary child and one very meagrely endowed intellectually.

One of the Mlles. Tardhivail has related the following facts : ' At that date, Bernadette often came to our house to receive writing lessons.   At the hospice they doubtless gave her some, but they rather neglected her because the Mother Superior had not got over her unpleasant impressions with respect to Bernadette.   [She did not do so until very much later.]   She had a horror of that little girl.' [1]

[1] R. P. Cros, *Histoire de Notre Dame de Lourdes*, t. II, p. 362.

Probably this estimate is extreme, but there is absolutely no doubt that the Superior of the hospice did not then believe in the apparitions, and did not do so until a long time afterwards. She saw Bernadette at too close quarters, and the latter's small exterior defects veiled her hidden, spiritual good qualities. The Abbé Pomian and Doctor Balencie are at one in saying: ' The Superior of the hospice, an intelligent woman, did not believe in the apparitions nor, consequently, in Bernadette's supernatural mission.' M. Peyramale, the parish priest, who had entrusted her to the care of the Sisters, tells us that a somewhat fiery medical man, doubtless Doctor Dozous, was a declared opponent of the Superior. ' Bernadette has been placed in bad hands,' he exclaimed; ' at all costs she must leave the hospice.' ' The great ground of (his) complaint,' adds M. Peyramale, ' is that this Sister does not believe in the apparitions at the grotto.'

Without putting absolute faith in these statements, we may nevertheless agree that the Superior, and the majority of the religious whom she ruled, did not need to make many meritorious efforts in order to humiliate and try Bernadette. Sister Victorine, in whose care she was, and whose excellent intentions and good faith we are not contesting in the least, writes: ' We tried to counterbalance all the homage Bernadette received by humiliating her before the very persons who were showing her honour.' These humiliations turned to Bernadette's advantage, in that they accustomed her to practise patience and, especially, to carry out her external mission, which was to edify and convince the visitors. For, adds the Sister, ' Never did Bernadette show either displeasure or ill-humour at the words we used under these circumstances in order to abase her, and she did not seem to remember them.' One day, two religious came and asked to see Bernadette at the hospice. 'Reverend Fathers,' said the Superior to them, ' before sending for the child, I scarcely venture to warn you to be prudent; but you know what a treasure I have to guard, and I prize Bernadette's humility as I do my eyesight. No compliments, I beg of you, and do not show too much admiration.' The Fathers questioned Bernadette and made her show them how our Lady had said: ' *I am the Immaculate Conception.*' ' I can still see Bernadette raising her eyes to heaven,' says one of the religious; ' a veritable image of the Blessed Virgin. Moreover, she said so simply: " Our Lady looked at me. . . . Our Lady spoke to me. . . ." I had no idea a heavenly favour could be borne with so peacefully. I was greatly impressed by this serenity. I saw there, and I still believe it, the first of the miracles of Lourdes.'

The Superior took note of the profound impression produced upon the visitors by Bernadette, for although they had said nothing flattering she thought they were not carrying out her instructions very well. ' Wait a moment, Reverend Fathers,' she said: ' Allow me to complete your information by telling you what the Blessed Virgin has not yet done for Bernadette, and that is convert her in earnest. With all these gratuitous graces, poor Bernadette is preparing some purgatory for herself, and you will be doing a work of charity in praying that she may improve. Would you believe it! just now, *Mademoiselle* and I had quite a discussion. She wanted to throw some peelings into a bucket on the right rather than into one on the left, and I foresaw the moment when I should have to give in to her.' ' Dear Mother,' said Bernadette on the instant, the tears in her eyes, ' again I beg your pardon.' This humility on the part of Bernadette, acknowledging her fault again and with tears, could only contribute still more to the edification of the two visitors, but the girl was not yet a saint; far from it.   She was not yet trained to the prompt and blind obedience of the religious, and the Reverend Mother was not altogether wrong in reprimanding her publicly.

M. Peyramale's treatment was no different and he showed her even less consideration. ' From the grotto,' writes the Abbé Delherm, ' we went to see the parish priest, who consented to send for Bernadette.   He treated her very harshly and I was really sorry for that child.   When she had gone, my uncle, Fr. Campardon, took the liberty of informing M. Peyramale how pained he had felt.   " If I treat her thus," replied the latter, " it is to preserve her from feelings of pride or conceit." '

Another priest tells of a precisely similar incident. He had been received at the presbytery, and Bernadette was awaited.   ' All at once,' relates the Abbé Néréci, ' the parlour opened and we saw before us a little peasant girl, frail and delicate in appearance, her head covered with a muslin scarf.   Her gentle face and limpid glance reflected the purity and innocence of her soul as in a mirror.

' " Here is the girl you were asking for," said the Curé. " The Blessed Virgin has shown her favours she does not deserve.   Many of her companions would have been more worthy of them."   The poor girl blushed, humbly bent her head, and bowing, without speaking a word, sat down on the chair offered her.'   Prejudiced in her favour by this modesty, the visitors questioned Bernadette.   One of them put some difficult, captious questions, to which she gave surprisingly apt replies, and that with a charming courtesy and simplicity which ended by disconcerting her opponent. A wealthy woman present wished to kiss her, and offered her money which she, of course, refused. The visitors went away completely won. Thus everything, even, and especially the trials, and the humiliations, contributed to exalt Bernadette. Such was not at all the way the visionaries of La Salette behaved. Maximin, in particular, was too easily annoyed and became impatient. M. Peyramale did not openly declare himself in favour of the visions. To those who asked him, he replied: 'Opinions are divided. For my own part, I am waiting until episcopal authority pronounces upon the matter.'

We say again: Let us not judge the conduct of the Sisters and the Curé too hardly. The attitude of Bernadette's best friend, her cousin, Jeanne Védère, then a school teacher at Momères, was not very different, yet she knew Bernadette well. 'Never,' she wrote—and this testimony is rather astonishing— 'did I notice that she was annoyed at anything. She always wanted what others wanted; she had no preference of her own.' Having brought Bernadette to Momères, with the permission of the parish priest and of the Bishop, M. Duffour came to photograph her. He said to Jeanne Védère: 'Bring a nice dress so that she can put it on before she poses.' When Bernadette learnt of this desire, she said: 'If M. Duffour does not think me nice enough, then let him leave me alone. If he wants the photograph to be of me, then let him be content with my dress. I will not put on one single pin in order to look more elegant.' The photographer wished to make the two girls pose together. Bernadette was pleased at this suggestion, and said to her cousin: 'When we have both entered religion, our relations will see us always together and that will please them.' It

was then that Jeanne, who was very fond of Bernadette, had an idea that seems very odd to us
to-day, but which shows well how those who were
constantly with the visionary were ever ready to
fear that the flattering attentions and veneration of
which she was the object would end by inspiring her
with feelings of vainglory. 'In order to mortify
her a little,' writes Jeanne, 'for I was always
afraid lest some conceited thought might be aroused
in her heart, owing to all the veneration in which
everybody held her, I replied: "Oh no! I don't
want to be exhibited in a shop window with
you." "You are right," she answered simply.'
Surprised at her frankness, Jeanne utters this reflection: 'I believe she never knew either self-love or
vanity.'[1]

All the witnesses who were familiar with Bernadette thought likewise, and yet, notwithstanding,
scarcely one among them failed to humiliate and try
her whenever an occasion presented itself. In every-
day life, Bernadette was very lively, cheerful, even
mischievous, blunt of speech, and they ended by
forgetting that she was our Lady's privileged child.
Fr. Sempé, who from the first to the eighth of
September, 1858, preached the retreat given to
the Children of Mary, to which sodality she then belonged, wrote: 'On the numerous occasions when
I have seen Bernadette I have always found her
equally humble, upright, and unsophisticated.'
Now the same excellent and experienced religious,
chancing to see her one day near the presbytery
coming away from a tiring and boring interrogation,
laughing and rubbing her hands for some little time,
whilst looking at the child who was with her, says:
'She was like a little schoolgirl, happy to come

[1] *Bernadette et Jeanne Védère*, p. 81.

out after being imprisoned in the class room. Already, though I believed in the apparitions at the grotto, I was somewhat scandalized at what I looked upon as a piece of mischief, and my faith in her was disturbed.'

So people whose minds were well-informed, but insufficiently aware that holiness may allow great liberty to the free play of the natural faculties, sometimes found Bernadette disconcerting. She was so, as we have seen, to the Superior of the hospice, who was a very virtuous and outstanding religious. She was no less so to Brother Léobard, head master of the boys' school at Lourdes, who had known her very intimately. He writes: 'At first sight, one might think that Bernadette was a very simple person indeed. Thus it was that many people who had seen her only in passing were mistaken about her. But as one watched her more closely it was soon evident that there was plenty of mischievous fun in her. The last time when, at my request, she came to relate to me again the story of all that had happened to her, I asked myself more than once, whilst observing her attentively, whether she were not rather a clever actress than an honest seer of visions; and I own to you that although I had always believed in the reality of the apparition, I should now be inclined to doubt it if the numerous cures which have taken place had not confirmed my conviction.'

Whereas passing pilgrims usually discerned Bernadette's supernatural characteristics at first sight, those who lived with her daily on familiar terms ended by seeing merely an ordinary little girl of the people. Let us add that she remained always childlike, especially as regards her stature and her gaiety. 'Bernadette,' wrote a Jesuit Father who came to visit her, ' is twenty-one years of age, but to believe this fact it is necessary to make an act of faith in the parish registers. She is still the child of thirteen of the time of the apparitions. I doubt whether it would be possible to find a child of thirteen who looks younger than Bernadette.'

Thus she looked like a little girl who had never developed, and it was possible to see in her something quite other than a very virtuous soul, who had seen visions and was destined to become a saint. Those who, *a priori* and unknown to themselves, had formed a too narrow idea of holiness ended inevitably by doubting as to her goodness.

As writes Père Cros, referring to this question: 'Brother Léobard and Père Sempé were worried over Bernadette's mischievous tricks, for such unbecoming behaviour might have fully justified the doubts and denials of serious-minded persons. In cases such as this, men have a right to look for perfectly consistent moral conduct in one who claims to be a messenger from God.' This opinion is fair and relatively true, but we must agree as to what is to be understood by 'unbecoming behaviour.'

Was it unbecoming behaviour to rub her hands with obvious satisfaction when she emerged from the presbytery after what had been a trying interview? Must we see this 'unbecoming behaviour' in the practical joke, so often related, when Bernadette, who carried a snuff box to relieve her asthma, passed it round the class room to her companions, and so caused frantic collective sneezing among the girls, to the great annoyance of the Sisters? Was there reason, on that account, to doubt of the apparitions and of Bernadette's very real virtues? Did this light-heartedness destroy the perfect moral harmony to be required in one who claims to be God's messenger? Obviously, if we confined ourselves exclusively to the

66   TRUE STORY OF ST. BERNADETTE

conception of sanctity suggested by the portrait of a
St. Aloysius, we should conclude with Père Cros that
Bernadette was nowhere on the road to sanctity.
But when we study the biographies of St. Philip Neri
and St. John Bosco, we are compelled to widen our
somewhat narrow, or Jansenist, ideas of holiness and
to form others that are much more human. Not
that we are denying in the least that, very exuberant
by nature, Bernadette did not need to be still corrected and disciplined. Physical sufferings and all
kinds of trials in the first place, then later on the
practices of religious discipline would provide for all
that. Only at that price would Bernadette become
really, and in every sense of the words, a great saint.

CHAPTER V

The Religious Vocation of Bernadette

IN the preceding chapter, we have shown at sufficient length, from the formal declarations of the most authentic witnesses, that Bernadette was not vulnerable to the more crude temptations to vanity as too many of those charged with her moral training feared. She was indifferent to the popular ovations, to the praises of visitors; but there are other, more subtle temptations of self-love and pride to which the girl might have been more liable. The majority of those who wrote the early story of the shrine of Our Lady of Lourdes do not record adequately how and to what an extent the real visions of Mary Immaculate to Bernadette were followed, during some months, by specious counterfeits, whereby the public might have been deceived.[1]

M. Peyramale was the first to believe in these 'apparitions,' and wrote to Mgr. Laurence, Bishop of Tarbes: 'The visions are still continuing. Last Thursday the maidservant at the Mayor's, a holy girl if ever there was one, seems to have seen the Blessed Virgin at the grotto. I sent for this girl, who is not my penitent, and she has promised me not to return to the grotto without my permission.' As Père Cros wisely remarks, the priest had never commended Bernadette as he had Marie Courrech: 'a holy girl if ever there was one.' The Abbé Serres, who was the confessor of this latter, and who also believed in the supernatural character of her

[1] *Histoire exacte des Apparitions de Lourdes à Bernadette.*

relevations, told her boldly: 'Go to the grotto.
You owe obedience to me and not to M. le Curé.'

Needless to say, we are in no way approving the
conduct of the Abbé Serres, but the fact explains how
the minds of many of the people of Lourdes were
already excited at this period, even among the priests.
M. Peyramale also spoke in favour of Marie Cazenave,
'a girl whose character offers every kind of satisfactory guarantee.' All the visionaries, for they were
numerous, did not inspire the same confidence.
Brother Léobard, the school master, writes: 'The
devil is raising up a countless number of visionaries,
and they may be seen giving themselves up to the
wildest extravagances. Several of my pupils claim to
have seen visions and are frequently absent from
school.'

Brother Céraze affirms likewise: 'A crowd of
small boys and girls was claiming to have seen our
Blessed Lady. I met some of them on the road
leading to the grotto, carrying candles in their hands
and kneeling beside the ponds.' The Brother adds:
'I began to have serious doubts with respect to the
visions of Bernadette.' Other excellent witnesses
whom we have met in an earlier work, such as
Dominica Vignes, Marie Portau, Dominiquette
Cazenave, Ursula Nicolau, state: 'Visionaries used
to come to the grotto; they seized the bunches of
fresh flowers which were brought there, and threw
them into the Gave, saying: "The Apparition does
not want flowers." One day a procession was seen
coming from the spring at Merlasse as far as the finger
post. Then one of them said: "All of you come
down with me. You are going to see our Lady."
Another cried out one night, already after nightfall:
"All of you say the rosary. The good God is
going to say it." Those present kissed the ground.'

We might multiply instances of this kind, but it would be wearisome, and even scandalous, and no doubt that is why writers of the history of Lourdes have abstained from recounting them. We should not have mentioned them ourselves, had it not been necessary, at least in a general way, to know that such scenes did take place, and that they were repeated during several months, in order to give readers an exact idea of the atmosphere of over-excitement at Lourdes. Mlle. Tardhivail writes: ' One cannot imagine to-day how credulous people living at Lourdes were at that time. Their imaginations were fired and they were unbalanced.'

It was as though a veritable spiritual storm, roused by Bernadette's visions, blew over Lourdes and piled up clouds; whilst the town was like a furnace, the many and violent flames of which were fanned by the gusts. Those who were the most level-headed and enlightened were themselves carried away. Jean-Baptiste Estrade confesses: ' The popular passion led us all astray.'

In such an atmosphere, Bernadette, the real visionary, might perhaps have been tempted to inter-vene. She might have lost her composure, her in-difference, at feeling she was distrusted, and been led to condemn the false visionaries loudly. She never allowed herself to be carried away by the slightest feeling of sensitiveness or self-love. She seemed to think it quite natural that M. Peyramale and his curates should prefer Marie Courrech and Marie Cazenave to herself. When visitors asked her: ' Are you the only one who has seen our Blessed Lady ? ' she answered modestly: ' They say that the maid at the Mayor's house has also seen her.' So her trans-cendent and really supernatural indifference never varied in the least. She soared far above the storm.

Once only did she seem to take sides in favour of those who had gone to the grotto in spite of the official prohibition. One of these had been condemned at Lourdes for having spread false reports concerning the opinions of the Emperor concerning the grotto. Cyprine Gesta had been condemned by the local magistrate's court at Lourdes. An appeal had been lodged at Pau. The culprit feared she would lose money or time. As she was about to leave, Bernadette said to her: ' Don't be afraid; nothing will happen.' In fact, she was acquitted. She returned to Lourdes and met Bernadette. ' The latter,' she says, ' was not a talker, for she never said three words where one would do. She simply called out, laughing: " I told you so." '

Had she been moved by an ambition which was, humanly speaking, legitimate and justified by seemingly supernatural motives, Bernadette might have exercised a great influence at Lourdes. She might have believed or claimed that she was inspired like St. Joan of Arc or St. Catherine of Siena; have given advice to those who approved of the grotto, put herself at the head of the quarrymen, imparted to the clergy or to her confessor the so-called inspired opinions she had conceived in prayer. It never entered into her head to fill such a rôle. She lived in an unalterable peace above the confusion of parties who, nevertheless, were warring for her or against her and over the happenings at the grotto. Very soon after the apparitions, she began to think more seriously than has been related of leaving Lourdes and becoming a contemplative nun.

Those who have read the work of Jean-Baptiste Estrade, very important for everything concerning the apparitions but far less reliable when he treats of Bernadette's vocation and religious life, conclude

quite naturally that she had never envisaged the
possibility of entering a religious congregation before
her interview with the Bishop of Nevers, Mgr.
Forcade. The latter had come to Lourdes on
September 25, 1863, and had been won to believe in
the apparitions since the decision thereon of the
Bishop of Tarbes and Lourdes. After having heard
Bernadette, however, his conviction was transformed
into enthusiasm and he thought of directing her to
the mother house of Nevers. According to Estrade,
the prelate introduced the subject of a vocation of
which Bernadette would never have thought, and
offered to secure her admission without a dowry to
the convent of Nevers. The girl replied: ' Before
committing myself, I want to think it over at length.'

The facts are quite otherwise. ' Soon after the
apparitions,' attests her godmother, ' Bernadette had
an idea of becoming a nun. She would have liked
to be a Carmelite, but it was explained to her that
her health would never allow of her entering that
order. However, she was not attracted to the Sisters
of Nevers.' The Abbé Pomian, chaplain to the
hospice and Bernadette's confessor and spiritual
director, states for his part that she would have liked
to join the Sisters of the Cross, and that the Sisters of
Nevers did not attract her. ' She conceived a liking
for the latter,' he adds, ' at the time when she was
devotedly nursing an old woman suffering from a
revolting illness.' The Sisters at the hospice also
agree in stating that from the time Bernadette came
to school with them as a boarder they noticed her
longing for the religious life. Consequently, there
can be no doubt that very soon after the apparitions
she thought very seriously of consecrating herself
entirely to God. It was a well-known fact at Lourdes,
and religious of divers congregations, who came on

pilgrimage to the grotto and visited her, invited her to join their institutes. Needless to say, on account of her celebrity, and of the outstanding graces which the Immaculate Mother had procured for her, Bernadette was a valuable recruit to a religious congregation, sickly and uneducated though she was. It was not so much the poor girl they sought to secure for themselves as the visionary. One day, a Sister of Charity took off her own cornette in order to put it on Bernadette's head. We may well imagine that such somewhat indiscreet proceedings were scarcely agreeable to the Sisters of the hospice.

Bernadette's cousin, of whom we have often spoken, Jeanne Védère, who was much older than she, was not made very welcome at the hospice either. She had a religious vocation, and they rather feared she might entice Bernadette away. ' Sister Gertrude ' (Jeanne Védère), writes her Prioress, ' is a right-minded person and does not take foolish ideas into her head. She thinks she noticed that the Sisters of Nevers at Lourdes did not view the frequent visits she paid to Bernadette with favour.' M. Peyramale was even obliged to intervene and order them never to refuse to allow Bernadette to see Jeanne, and to leave them alone together so that they could talk over their pious aspirations to the religious life. Sister Marie, who was told to look after Bernadette, said to Jeanne Védère, who tells us of the incident: ' " So you want to be a nun ? " " Yes, Sister." " Come to us." I smiled and answered: " I feel no attraction to be a Sister of Nevers." Sister Marie, who bore a very lively and tender affection for Bernadette, began to cry, and said: " Do not take Bernadette with you." " My good Sister," I replied, " you need not cry. My cousin will never enter anywhere because of me. Bernadette will not leave the ladies of Nevers." "Do you think that?" asked the Sister. "Yes, you may be tranquil." '

It is from Jeanne Védère that we learn the most precious details concerning Bernadette's vocation. The former's vocation was opposed by her relatives, and these had asked Bernadette to dissuade her cousin from entering the religious life. Bernadette informed Jeanne of the reasons put forward by her family, but did not dissuade her in the least. This took place in 1860. Jeanne then asked Bernadette to pray for her. ' The first time I saw her after this conversation,' she writes, ' I asked her if she had thought of me. After a moment's reflection, she replied: " Yes. You must be patient; you will succeed, but not yet." ' This assurance on Bernadette's part, which savours rather of a prophetic utterance, gives one to think. Had Bernadette supernatural revelations during her mental or vocal prayer? We might believe so. At this time, Jeanne wanted to enter first among the Sisters of St. Vincent de Paul, with the intention of subsequently passing over to the Carmelites. Bernadette replied at once: ' See that you do not do so on any account.' On this subject, writes her cousin, ' she rebuked me as a highly experienced spiritual director might have done. " It is," she said, " as though you intended to deceive both God and man, and God does not allow Himself to be deceived. It is He who is giving you the attraction to the cloister, but it is not He who is giving you the idea of entering with the Sisters of St. Vincent de Paul with the intention of leaving them later on. Believe me, God sees the difficulties and permits them, and He will know how to make everything smooth when the time comes." ' Bernadette's thoughts were, indeed, perfectly wise, albeit at seventeen she looked

like a girl of thirteen. They remind us of the
words of M. Vène, who tested the waters of the
Pyrenees, a man of great learning and earnest piety.
' In that child, I saw both great simplicity and pre-
cocious good judgement.' Bernadette was by no
means the unintelligent little shepherdess which
some biographies portray for us. Let us repeat,
moreover, that when dealing with spiritual matters
she seemed to have been really favoured with supernatural light. Three years later, she declared to her
cousin, with regard to the latter's vocation: ' The
greatest obstacle will soon vanish.' The godmother
of Jeanne, who more than anyone else had been
opposing her vocation, died shortly afterwards.
Bernadette remarked at the time: ' Your poor godmother has soon died. I assured you that the chief
difficulty would soon disappear. It was to her that
I was referring.'

We have related all these details concerning the
vocation of Jeanne Védère in order to emphasize
both the wisdom and the supernatural inspiration
which governed all Bernadette's decisions. It has
been sufficiently shown how truly she was a wise
virgin, directed by a sort of instinct where divine
things were concerned. We now proceed to treat
of her own vocation, and we shall there find the same
inspired prudence.

' My cousin,' Jeanne writes again, ' had not yet
spoken to me of her own vocation. It was then, in
1861, that she did so for the first time.' Bernadette
was magnanimous, and spontaneously her first choice
had fallen upon one of the most austere and contemplative of the religious Orders. It was a question of
nothing less than the Reformed Cistercians, or
Trappistines. How had the girl come to know of
this Order? The question has been asked, and the

thing seems so mysterious that some have thought that our Lady must have revealed it to her. We do not think anything of the kind. That profound religious instinct, of which we have spoken in Bernadette's case, and which has been far too little recognized, led her to find out the most hidden realities when they corresponded to the deepest inspirations of her soul. She greatly loved Saint Bernard. By this time, she could read, and, led by a wholly spiritual curiosity, she had been able to read lives of the great saint and to obtain information about the religious who were under his protection.

' She could not praise sufficiently,' writes Jeanne, ' a religious Order of which I had never heard. She told me what they did in this Order; she talked of the fasts, the vigils, the disciplines, the mortifications. " I should like that very much, if I had a little health," she said.' What completed Bernadette's attraction to the Cistercians was the strict enclosure that separated these nuns from the world. ' Nobody would come to pester me there ! ' So we may sum up her religious ideal under two heads : rigorous asceticism on the one hand, and contemplative life on the other. She had thought very seriously of entering that Order. Very probably, she had also questioned her confessor, her parish priest or other competent persons. ' I was told,' she added, ' that they would not accept me because I had such poor health.'

Whenever she saw her cousin, she talked again of this Order she so loved, and which our Lady loved too, and earnestly advised her to enter it. The Abbé Portalet, to whom the girls came to pay a visit, offered them medals of St. Benedict. When they were leaving, Bernadette said : ' In the religious Order of which I have talked so much, they follow the Rule of St. Benedict,' and she held forth on the characteristics of the Cistercians until some persons came to interrupt her conversation. We might well be astonished that Bernadette, at eighteen, had studied in such detail the Cistercian Order of which her cousin, a school teacher at Momères and over thirty years of age, knew nothing whatever, and which the latter was later to enter; but predestined souls are often guided more infallibly, and more promptly, by intuitions and instinct than by patient, intellectual research.

However, Bernadette was too wise not to give heed to the advice of those who told her not to think of an austere, contemplative order on account of her health, but she then no longer knew what course to take. She felt no attraction to the Congregation of Nevers, and she waited.

Moreover, just at this time she was very ill. On April 30, 1862, she had an attack of pneumonia, all the more serious in that it was a relapse. The Sisters reproached themselves for having allowed her to go to the grotto, where they thought she had caught a cold. Her condition became worse and a medical consultation was judged necessary. The doctors were at one in deciding that she was doomed to die, and that almost immediately. Bernadette was given the Last Sacraments in all haste, and with all sorts of precautions. She was constantly coughing, and could then scarcely breathe. In order that she might communicate, she was given only a small fragment of the Host, and to enable her to swallow it more easily they made her take a few drops of Lourdes water. Then a kind of miracle took place. Bernadette declared she was cured. She felt relieved, ' as though a mountain had been lifted from her chest.' All the alarming symptoms disappeared during the following night, so completely that she herself received

M. Balencie, the doctor who attended the hospice, in the parlour. After a moment's amazement, the doctor attributed the cure to the efficacy of the remedies he had ordered. M. Peyramale notes as regards this subject that, to the doctor's great embarrassment, the remedy prescribed had not been applied, and that, further, there had been a sudden recovery without convalescence. It is the solitary occasion, so far as we know, upon which Bernadette was cured or relieved by the intervention of Our Lady of Lourdes. Moreover, as she declared to a pilgrim, she had never asked for her cure. The mysterious and supernatural intuition by which she was guided gave her a presentiment that her vocation was to be a willing victim, and that although she had still some years of life they would not pass without keen sufferings.

Indeed she was constantly ill during the two following years. ' She then went through all sorts of maladies and pains,' Sister Victorine tells us; ' toothache, rheumatic pains, haemorrhages and blood spitting, palpitation of the heart, constant oppression frequently caused by such violent attacks of asthma that we had to carry her to the window to enable her to breathe; and in her agony she would cry: " Open my chest ! " '

The daughter of the Subirous could stand a great deal of pain; our Lady's witness was exceptionally courageous. Although she was hardly ever free from suffering, those who knew her most intimately perceived nothing of it. She never complained, unless it were during the most violent seizures, and even then she showed no sign of impatience.

In the summer of 1863, M. Fabisch came to Lourdes to make a statue of *Our Lady of Lourdes*, according to Bernadette's description, destined for the grotto. He recognized that the girl's chest was very seriously affected; she was already suffering from tuberculosis which was spreading through her whole body, and when he returned to Lourdes on March 30, 1864, he found Bernadette in bed. 'This interesting child,' he writes, ' has been very ill for some days; so ill that we feared we should lose her. She is confined to bed, very resigned and very edifying, and could not be present at the celebration.' The solemn blessing of the statue in the arched niche of the grotto took place on April 4; the weather was very fine and the ceremony was splendid. Setting out from the parish church, the procession took the road to Massabieille, Mgr. Laurence, Bishop of Tarbes, presiding. The crowd was enormous. ' The windows,' as the newspapers reported, 'were crowded with people; garlands of ivy and box were stretched from house to house. The walls were draped with white material, decorated with stars or inscriptions. A multitude was massed in the surrounding streets, and especially in front of the grotto. When His Lordship let fall the veil covering the statue, only piety restrained the people from cheering, and the Bishop then blessed it.'

Bernadette was in bed, somewhat recovered from a fresh attack that had caused grave anxiety. M. Peyramale would on no account allow her to get up and be taken to the grotto, even in a carriage. Jeanne Védère was present at the ceremony. ' There was something so moving in this procession. One had to see it to form an idea of it.' When she arrived at Lourdes, she went straight to the hospice to visit her cousin. She expressed her regret that the latter was unable to be present at the ceremony. Bernadette replied: ' I am as pleased to remain in this bed as I should be if I could go to the grotto.

I was impatiently awaiting this lovely day. I wanted to see that beautiful procession and also the statue of the Blessed Virgin in her niche. God wills me to see nothing of all that. May His holy will be done! I shall be at the grotto with everyone in spirit, since I cannot go otherwise. Do not pity me, for when we are doing what God wills we are not to be pitied.' [1]

M. Peyramale was not present at this ceremony either. He was ill; so much so that his condition was arousing acute uneasiness. In his important work on Our Lady of Lourdes, the Abbé Moniquet recalls how indignant the parish priest had been when Bernadette had come to tell him on behalf of our Lady: ' I wish that they should come in procession.' He was tied to his bed, and perhaps that was, remarks the author, ' a special token of friendship on the part of the Apparition towards a recent friend!' [2] Be that as it may, a week later the Curé of Lourdes was able to write to his Bishop: ' Thank God the progress of my convalescence has been as rapid as it was unhoped for. To-day (April 10) I have had the happiness of saying holy Mass and giving my conference to the congregation.'

Bernadette was not so ill but that, strictly speaking, she might not have been taken to Massabieille, provided that all precautions had been taken. Sister Vincent Garros had heard her affirm that with her own lips. In her frank but blunt speech, Bernadette had said: ' Monseigneur Peyramale had forbidden me to take part in the procession, but our Blessed Lady held him fast. She sent him a good dose of colic which prevented him from being present himself.' [3]

[1] *Bernadette et Jeanne Védère*, p. 74.
[2] *La Divine Histoire de Notre-Dame de Lourdes*, p. 162.
[3] *Summary of the Process of Canonization*, p. 64.

We wish and believe that M. Peyramale, although very easily roused, was as resigned as Bernadette. For her privileged clients, our Lady has marks of attention which, from a human standpoint, are surprising. All the same, it was difficult to be as 'abandoned' to the divine will as Bernadette already was. About this time, a pilgrim who had planned to visit Spain wrote: 'I have seen the grotto of Lourdes; I have seen Bernadette; I neither wish to, nor can I see anything more. In her I have seen one of the purest and most moving creations in the mystical order.' This visitor, who wrote to M. Peyramale from Biarritz, voiced a thought that was already true but which would be realized in the future in a more important manner than he thought.

In September, 1863, Mgr. Forcade, Bishop of Nevers, came to Lourdes and found that Bernadette's health had much improved during the summer months. He came to visit her at the Sisters' hospice. When he arrived, Bernadette was ringing the bell with all her might to announce his coming. As he passed her, the prelate said: 'Prou! Prou! Prou!' which in the local patois means: 'Enough! Enough! Enough!' Bernadette, whom all her companions describe as gay and cheerful, laughed heartily, saying: 'His Lordship can speak patois!' She went to the kitchen and set to work to scrape carrots. Going over the hospice, Mgr. Forcade passed through the kitchen, but did not say a word to her then. Some time afterwards, he sent for her to the parlour. He talked to her of her vocation, remarking that she could not expect to remain always with the Sisters of Nevers as a pupil, and asked her whether she had not thought of entering among them as a religious. Bernadette replied that she had no dowry, that she was often ill, and then added: 'I know nothing and am good for nothing.' The Bishop replied: 'I have seen that you are at least good at scraping carrots.' 'Oh,' rejoined Bernadette, laughing, 'that is not difficult.' The Bishop assured her that she could be received at Nevers without a dowry and employed in the kitchen or elsewhere. The interview ended by her making this statement: 'I will think about it, but I have not yet decided.' In fact, whether owing to circumstances or in order to consider her plan thoroughly before God, the girl had to wait another two years. Soon illness laid her low again. A priest who visited her on April 14, 1864, writes: 'Bernadette lives at the hospice. This pious child has been entrusted to the Sisters. At present she is very ill, and will probably soon die. I was greatly struck by her modesty and by her patience under violent attacks of coughing. She never once raised her eyes to me, and there was no sort of constraint in this reserve. I blessed her, and I noticed how she recollected herself and quietly made the Sign of the Cross, whilst doing her best to stifle the noise of her rapid breathing.'

Winter and the early days of spring were the critical season for Bernadette, as is the case with the majority of tubercular patients. It was April. Seeing her so ill, the pilgrim believed her death imminent, but there was an astonishing vitality in her. In a few days she would seem literally to have risen from a death bed. We shall see a memorable example. Naturally very energetic, upheld moreover by grace, she would rise immediately she felt better, and at once resume her daily occupations.

The summer of 1864 was very favourable to her. In September, the Abbé Pomian wrote to the Sisters of Ste. Chrétienne at Metz: 'Bernadette's health is greatly improved. Notwithstanding the fatigue caused by having to receive visitors continually, her condition is very satisfactory.' It was in the month of October that she came to spend six weeks at Momères with her cousin. She talked at length with her about her vocation, and she was already preparing herself for the religious life by increasing piety and regularity. ' She was very exact in following her little rule of life,' Jeanne Védère tells us; ' she went to Mass daily and to Holy Communion three times in the week. Every evening she made a visit to the Blessed Sacrament, and every day she said her rosary. In the village and the neighbourhood she was very much liked by all. She was cheerful and lively, and was very fond of joking with one of her boy cousins. This tendency to let herself go when with her intimate friends, which was one of the outstanding traits of Bernadette's character, might have led to serious harm, and she would still have to correct herself of it.

On her return to Lourdes, she announced to the Superior of the hospice that she had decided to enter the Congregation of the Sisters of Nevers, and from that time onwards she set herself to observe their Rule more faithfully. Nevertheless, the constant stream of visitors, who were a cause of distraction to her, tried her very much. After ill-timed conversations, the Sisters often heard her exclaim: ' Oh, how these ladies plague me ! ' The pilgrim who relates this expression thinks well to remark that it is the only one known to the common people. Bernadette, no doubt, knew another, but she did not hesitate to use strong language.

On May 21, 1866, took place the solemn opening of the crypt. This time Bernadette was able to take part in the procession. ' She wore her dress as a Child of Mary,' says Jeanne Védère, ' and looked as beautiful as an angel.' Bernadette said to her cousin: ' Come with us; otherwise you will not be able to see anything or to hear the sermon. You will stay beside me.' Jeanne was not dressed in white like the Children of Mary, and did not want to make herself conspicuous. The Sisters wanted to lend her a white dress and, on her refusal, proposed to dress her up in their habit. They said no one would pay any attention to her and would take her for one of the hospice Sisters. ' Knowing that Bernadette was present, after the procession the pilgrims all wanted to see her, so that the Sisters and her companions had to surround her in order to shield her from the indiscreet veneration of the devotees of Our Lady of Lourdes.'

When talking with her cousin, Bernadette told her: ' Since I have not sufficient health to enter where I should have liked, I shall stay here. I am very fond of the Sisters of St. Vincent de Paul, but I should not have the courage to hurt the Sisters of Nevers. Oh, it is not on account of my poor person that they are anxious for me to stay. I understand that quite well, for I shall be of no use. What would you have them do with me ? I like looking after sick people; I shall remain. They have looked after me for a long time and I ought to be grateful.' We see from these words, spoken in the early summer of 1866, that Bernadette had made up her mind. She would enter with the Sisters of Nevers. On June 15 of the same year, she wrote to a Sister:

' My dear Mother,
          ' I am happy to let you know that I have at last decided to enter our dear congregation. How glad I should be, Mother, if I could see you, but I believe that it will be difficult since I am

pressed for time, having to settle my business.   I am
hoping to set out at the beginning of next month.'

Bernadette did, in fact, leave Lourdes on July 4,
1866.   Estrade has told us in detail of her last visit
to the grotto, in a long passage which we abbreviate:
' On the day before her departure she went to
Massabieille, accompanied by two or three religious
from the hospice.   At the sight of the hallowed spots
she burst out sobbing, went up to the rock above
which is the niche, and pressed her lips to it several
times.   The Sisters softly approached and told her
it was time to leave.   As the girl, her face bathed in
tears, could with difficulty drag herself away from the
blessed places she would never see again, one of the
Sisters said to her: " But, Bernadette, why are you
grieving like this ?   Do you not know, surely, that
our Lady is everywhere, and that everywhere she
will be your mother ? "   " Oh yes, I know," she
answered, " but at Lourdes the grotto was my
heaven ! " '

The religious had said to Bernadette just what
came into her mind.   We might criticize her reflection.   If our Lady is everywhere, and everywhere
shows herself equally our mother, it might be objected
that it is of no use to go on pilgrimage to Lourdes.
In fact, we must recognize that under the circumstances one could scarcely say anything else than
what the good Sister said.   A confessor of Bernadette,
who was an enlightened spiritual director, and who
had explained to her some time previously the
reason why our Lady might see fit to call her to
Nevers, could then in a few words remind her that
her mission as interpreter at Lourdes was finished,
and that it remained for her to give a very great, and
almost unique example of abnegation and detachment.

The Lourdes grotto was indeed a spot blessed beyond others. There Bernadette had received extraordinary graces, and devout pilgrims would come to kneel before the statue of the Immaculate Conception, drink from the miraculous spring, and there obtain also outstanding graces; but the grotto of Lourdes was not necessary to the Christian faith. Precisely because she had there been the privileged child of our Lady, it was necessary that Bernadette should set an outstanding example of self-abnegation. Thenceforth, her vocation would be to become a saint, and a victim, praying and doing penance for the salvation of sinners. It was in the Congregation and in the Mother-House of the Sisters of Nevers that she would be made perfect; that, aided by grace, she would learn how to reach the highest sanctity, and that she would also fulfil her destiny as a victim.

On the next day, the girl who, by her visions, was to cause innumerable throngs to hasten to Lourdes from every corner of the globe, left her native town never to return.

CHAPTER VI

BERNADETTE ENTERS THE CONVENT OF NEVERS

BERNADETTE left Lourdes on the morning of July 4, with a companion, Léontine Muret, and the Superior of the hospice, and arrived the same evening at Bordeaux. It was a Wednesday, and they spent two days in seeing the city. Bernadette has left us in a letter the record of her impressions:

' They made us visit all the houses, including the *Institution Impériale*, which could be called rather a palace than a religious house. It is not like that at Lourdes. We went to see the Carmelite church, and from there we made our way to the Garonne to see the ships. We also went to the botanical gardens. We saw something novel there; guess what? Fish, red, black, white and grey. What I thought nicest of all was to see these little creatures swimming without being afraid whilst a crowd of mischievous little boys was watching them.'

Here Bernadette makes a remark apparently naïve, but in reality more significant than might be thought when glancing cursorily through her letter. She was herself an object of curiosity to very many people belonging to all classes of society. She was telling herself that to maintain an attitude of absolute indifference beneath the eyes of men, as did the fish in the botanical gardens of Bordeaux, was something rare and to be envied.

On Friday, July 6, they left Bordeaux, slept the night at Perigueux, and the next morning took the ten o'clock train for Nevers, which was reached at

half-past ten at night. The two postulants were
taken to the convent of Saint Gildard, and almost
immediately to the common dormitory. Bernadette
scarcely slept at all, and owns that during the following
day both she and her companion rarely ceased from
crying. 'The good Sisters encouraged us by telling
us it was a sign of vocation.' In most of her biographies, we are told that Bernadette had generously
made the sacrifice of Lourdes and the grotto, and
that relatively easily. Such is not quite the case.
'I am able to state,' says one religious during the
Process of Canonization, 'that during the first days
Sister Marie-Bernard spent at Nevers, she grieved
very much, and was often crying. I asked her why
she was sad, and she replied that she missed her
visits to the grotto very much, and did not think she
could become used to this privation.'

Bernadette was well received at the convent of
Saint Gildard. In the annals of the noviciate, we
read: 'At last our longings are fulfilled! Bernadette
is among us! She is just as she has been depicted
for us: humble in her supernatural triumph, smiling
and quietly happy; although her frail, delicate body
has long been undermined by sickness.' In the
presence of the whole community, the Mother-
General of the Congregation asked her to tell the
story of the apparitions, which she did with the
greatest simplicity, as she was wont to do, and
answered all the questions put to her. After this
lengthy recital, the novices and postulants were
formally forbidden to speak to her thenceforth about
the happenings at Lourdes and her visions. This
strict order was rigorously and scrupulously obeyed.
Bernadette and—what is more surprising—her companions in the noviciate maintained absolute silence
upon this attractive subject. The Bishop of Nevers,

Mgr. Forcade, writes: 'I do not hesitate to declare that this, seemingly insignificant, little incident was heroic.' It gives us a high opinion of the observance and regularity practised at the Mother-House and in the noviciate of the Sisters of Nevers.

The Congregation of the Sisters of Charity and Christian Instruction of Nevers had been founded in the second half of the seventeenth century by a Benedictine, Dom de Laveyne. The mere word 'Benedictine' might evoke to our imagination the figure of a monk living in a great, organized monastery among his brethren, but there was nothing of all that about him. No doubt Dom de Laveyne had imbibed from the monastic traditions of his Order the love of the liturgy and of the interior life, but he lived alone in the priory of Saint-Saulge, not far from Nevers. He led a life analogous to that of a good parish priest, and he maintained the celebration of Catholic liturgical worship in the church which he had repaired and embellished. He was, moreover, a real monk, but he directed his penitents of both sexes towards the works of charity which were to be seen developing everywhere at the end of the seventeenth century. He had trained a chosen group of young people, to whom he had given the name of 'apostles,' who devoted themselves entirely to good works. The model of these apostles at Saint-Saulge was M. Paillard, a distinguished barrister. He lived in the world but devoted himself to the poor whom he visited, and to the children whom he gathered together in order to teach them the classics.

Dom de Laveyne also directed a group of young women whom he led to occupy themselves in charitable undertakings. Among these were Anne Lejay and Marie de Marchengy, who were subsequently to become the first collaborators of which he made use

to found the Congregation of Sisters of Charity of
Nevers. The first foundation was made at Saint-
Saulge, where Dom de Laveyne established the little
community in one room. Under his guidance, the
two led a life of recollection and union with God;
they also followed a rule of life like nuns. At first,
they were known as ' Sisters of Mercy.' They visited
the hovels of the poor and the sick in order to look
after them and distributed material assistance. The
simple folk called them the ' Sisters of the soup
cauldron!' They set up a small school at Saint-
Saulge and taught the first elements of sacred and
profane instruction to the children of the poor. Won
by their ideal of self-sacrifice and Christian life, some
other girls joined them, so that they soon numbered
eight or ten. Among these, there was one, Marcelline
Pauper, who set such an extraordinary example of
prayer, mortification, and apostolic labour, that she
would always be for the Sisters of Nevers the veritable
ideal of the form of religious life which they were
called upon to practise.

Marcelline Pauper who, at the bidding of our
Lord Himself, imitated St. Catherine of Siena, who
was her patron, practised penance in a degree that
appears excessive to us now. ' My sister, Marcelline,'
St. Catherine had said to her, ' you must fortify
yourself with great courage, for we must attain to
Jesus Christ glorified by way of Jesus Christ crucified.
Be sure to remember this way. You must go by
Jesus Christ suffering.'

To anticipate events: the life of Marcelline
Pauper appeared in 1871, published at Nevers, and
became a bedside book for the Sisters. At that date,
Bernadette had been five years at Saint Gildard, and
we are told that she loved to read and re-read lives of
the saints. Hence she read also that of Marcelline

Pauper, who is set before all her Sisters as a living model. She would retain—for nothing could be more in accordance with her destiny and her mission —the principle that we attain to Christ glorified by way of Christ crucified.[1]

Not but, to use that time-honoured expression, many of the practices of Marcelline Pauper are to be admired rather than imitated, especially in our day. She took the discipline daily; she wore an iron girdle; her director, Dom de Laveyne, having procured for her a crown with iron points, she put it on her head and kept it there for six months on end. She wore a hairshirt of the roughest kind which ' ate away her flesh on her side,' and which she removed fearing a surgeon might have to be summoned. Bernadette did nothing of that kind.

In Marcelline Pauper, we find a great attraction to prayer. She would remain rapt therein for whole hours; she lived consciously in the presence of God day and night, and during the most absorbing occupations. ' The presence of God had become so familiar to me,' she wrote in the account of her life,[2] ' that it was as easy to think of God as to breathe. . . . My busy occupations did not hinder me from attending to God, so that I lived in continual recollection.' Marcelline was, in fact, sent to make several foundations. From the first, in particular, which was made at Decize, she was sent to Murat in Auvergne. It was when she reached the latter town that she offered herself to God ' as a victim desiring to be immolated to His glory.' ' I own,' she adds, ' that from that

---

[1] Bernadette writes : ' Way to write in my heart the name of . . .' This way merely consists in writing the names of our Lord and the saints to whom she has vowed a very special devotion. Among these, we find St. Martha, St. Bernard, and then Marcelline Pauper. (*Sainte Bernadette*, par Chanoine Lemaître, p. 57.)

[2] *Vie de Marcelline Pauper*, écrite par elle-même, Nevers, 1871.

time I have felt an over-mastering passion to be made conformable to Jesus crucified.' She was subsequently Superior of the house at Nevers for two years. Bernadette will strive to her utmost, and that more and more, to know only Jesus crucified, and her quite special vocation will be to be a victim. In that, she will equal Marcelline Pauper, but it will suffice for her to accept the sufferings and trials which God will send her.

Studying the life of Marcelline Pauper, the reader is astonished, as we have said, at the extraordinary and even odd practices of mortification, and by the gift of prayer which rendered it relatively easy for her to be united to God by day and by night; but he is no less surprised at the life of activity and the intense apostolic spirit which she showed, and especially when making her foundations. Equal to all sorts of labour, even the most ordinary, such as baking bread, lighting the stove, milking cows, cleaning the stables; and at the same time apt for the highest, she undertook even those that would seem to be reserved to priests and male religious. At Saint Etienne, she gave a retreat to forty-eight girls with the greatest success. Without being prepared for it, she gave the conferences with a facility that surprised even herself. 'Although for a number of years now, I have no longer been able to apply myself to discursive meditation, I did it all aloud and with so much unction that all the girls dissolved in tears.' Moreover, she devoted the time that remained to her to seeing them and advising them on spiritual matters. 'God put into my mouth what I had to say to each one, in such wise that they were all consoled.' Such was the apostolic zeal for souls in the case of one of the first and holiest of the foundresses of the Congregation of the Sisters of

Nevers. It derived its source from, and was wholly inspired by, an interior life of prayer.

The Sisters of Nevers have been faithful in practising this harmonious life which includes, at the same time, prayer, study, and active work; they are both con-templatives and active religious. Without being bound to the recitation of any office in private, their rule of life is so carefully drawn up that it secures always the larger share for prayer, spiritual reading, the chanting of the liturgical offices and meditation. Owing to force of circumstances, it resulted that Bernadette, forced by illness to abstain from active good works, there led the kind of life which she had first sought as her ideal: a life of suffering and con-templation.

Another providential reason that may have counted for something in Bernadette's decision to enter among the Sisters of Nevers, has been pointed out by several writers. At Saint-Saulge, wishing to give the Sisters a more suitable house, Dom de Laveyne had acquired the *Hôtel de la Croix blanche*. Beside the hotel was a house of amusement, and he bought that also. There he built a church which was the first in the diocese of Nevers to be dedicated to the Immaculate Conception. Did not this cultus for Mary Immaculate, emphasized so markedly from the first days of the congregation, contribute to merit that the chosen child of Our Lady of Lourdes should enter therein?

After the first sad days she went through at the memory of Lourdes and the grotto, Bernadette settled down very quickly to religious life in the Mother-House. She felt at home and as though she were in a new family. Let us point out this detail, which has its importance. The congregation has no lay sisters. That does not mean, of course, that all the religious are destined indifferently to teach and do housework, but all wear the same habit and have the same rights. Bernadette must have gained greatly from this spirit of sisterly charity. She wrote to the Lourdes Sisters: ' I assure you that if I had to leave our dear noviciate now, the sacrifice would be very bitter. One feels one is in God's house. One must love it in spite of oneself, so I never cease to address my poor prayers to our Lord to thank Him for all the graces He never ceases to shower upon me.'

Bernadette received the habit on July 29, 1866, about three weeks after her arrival. The ordinary period of postulancy had been much shortened for her, but they had reckoned as such the period spent with the Sisters at Lourdes, when she had followed the rule as far as she could. On her Clothing day, she received the name of Sister Marie-Bernard, by which we shall henceforth call her.

' I had the happiness,' attests Sister Emilienne Marcillac, ' to receive the holy habit with Sister Marie-Bernard. I was impressed by the way she made her retreat. How recollected she was ! Nothing that happened around her was capable of distracting her.' The noviciate therefore began for Sister Marie-Bernard in a manner that raised the highest hopes. From the first, she had understood the importance of regular observance, and she set herself to keep her rule every day as perfectly as possible.

It is time to examine in detail how Bernadette will create for herself the fundamental elements of her own religious life. In every religious institute, the novice always begins by practising the exercises of the ascetic life. Except in cases where exceptional graces are bestowed, the mystical life, properly speaking, will develop only subsequently.

Usually the beginner does not escape falling into exaggerations—very excusable, especially when they are not contrary to obedience. Bernadette had already too much experience of the Christian life and, moreover, too much common sense to fall into such excesses. One fast day, her cousin Jeanne Védère went down to the grotto in the forenoon, and stayed there until three in the afternoon without taking any food. When Bernadette heard of it, she was rather annoyed. ' Oh, see,' she commented, ' she is going to the good God by the way of fear instead of by that of love. You believe that God is very harsh, and He is so good! There! He would have been better pleased with you if you had eaten something. Another time, if you come fasting I will not go to the grotto with you.' This anecdote—which is quite true, for it is related by Jeanne herself—is significant, for it shows that, shortly before she entered the convent, Bernadette was disposed, owing to a certain broadmindedness and large-heartedness, not to observe the letter of the law in too absolute a manner. Yet she was to be a novice rigorously faithful to her rule and, in particular, observant of silence. ' Very exact in observing the rule, she was especially so in keeping silence,' witnesses Sister Vincent Garros. ' Sometimes I approached her to ask her for something in silence time, and she fled from me as though I had the plague.' Another Sister speaks similarly, but adds a corrective that well shows how balanced were Bernadette's faculties. ' Sister Marie-Bernard was strict in the observance of silence, but at recreation she was pleasant to talk to and possessed a witty humour.' All her biographers relate the following anecdote: When she came to recreation on one of the first days after her entrance into the noviciate, she asked whether they skipped, and when answered in the negative, remarked: ' Oh, what a pity! At Lourdes I loved turning the skipping-rope for my companions to jump.' Sister Marie-Bernard saw nothing unbecoming in novices skipping during recreation. To be sure, few religious of her time shared her opinion; some must have been even a little scandalized, or at least astonished at the novice's remark and thought her boisterous. We share Bernadette's opinion.

Nearly all her companions have noted that she did not practise extraordinary fasts and abstinence. As one tells us: ' She gave to sleep the time laid down by the rule. One of the most outstanding characteristics of her asceticism was her absolute submission to rule.' In his notes, the Abbé Febvre, the chaplain, emphasizes ' the fidelity of Sister Marie-Bernard in the smallest things.' This fidelity at once reminds us of St. Teresa of the Child Jesus. Both saints followed by preference, in their pious practices and in their penances, what has been called the asceticism of little things. Sister Josephine Forestier states: ' Many of the nuns took her (Bernadette) for a model.' Another religious tells us: ' During the time I spent in the noviciate with Sister Marie-Bernard, her humility, her simplicity, her obedience and her regularity were so great that it was impossible to imitate her. I tried several times, putting all my good will into it, but I could never reach her standard. The fact was the novice was studying every means whereby to convince herself of the importance of regular life.' ' She was very fond of spiritual reading,' we are told, ' she made notes, she carefully studied the Rule, re-reading it often in order to practise it more faithfully.'

They tell us that great mortifications did not attract her, but she sought after little sacrifices. ' She refrained from drinking when she was thirsty, often waiting an hour, or an hour and a half, before doing so. In the refectory, she was continually mortifying her natural preferences. Her fellow religious noticed that she always took what she most disliked. When ill and taking medicines, the more bitter they were the more she smiled. She always accepted the reprimands and observations made to her.'

In submitting herself to obedience, she was minutely exact. Thus she refused to sign a pious picture because she had not obtained permission. ' She was especially conspicuous,' another tells us, ' by her promptness in going to her duties at the first sound of the bell. At recreation someone quoted as characteristic of a certain Benedictine that, on hearing the bell, he left a letter unfinished. " That is not difficult," she remarked.' It was clear to all that she did likewise.

It would be superfluous to multiply examples. Those we have given suffice to show that the novice was firmly resolved to set out on the road to holiness. Let us remember also that she was never guilty of exaggeration, and above all avoided singularity. As Sister Emilienne Marcillac testifies: ' There was one novice who was always closing her eyes. " Look at her," said Bernadette, " she is always shutting her eyes, and if she had not her companion to lead her some accident would happen to her. Why shut our eyes when we need to keep them open ? " ' Bernadette's good sense and perfect balance protected her instinctively from such exaggerations in her behaviour.

It must not be thought that this precision in the smallest matters, this constant submission of her will, cost her nothing. She had often to do violence to herself. ' By continually whacking the beast,' she used to say, ' you end by mastering it.' As regards what concerns the practice of the humble religious

virtues, when she left Lourdes Bernadette was not
yet a saint. It was above all when she came to
Nevers that she began to scale the rough path of
perfection and sanctity. The reflection of Sister
Marcelline Durand, who knew her well, is very
suggestive and quite accurate. 'I have often thought,
and I have said that if Bernadette had not seen our
Lady, and received her heavenly graces, the virtues
of which she set the example would be sufficient to
canonize her.' In the latter's notebook, we may
read a resolution that gives us to think: 'I must be
a great saint; Jesus wills it.' It was a long and
painful task which the novice undertook, and which
she did not achieve without long efforts and without
bearing terrible trials.

As we have said, sickness had worn her out since
her childhood and brought her to death's door. She
had even received the Last Sacraments at Lourdes.
Only three months after she had received the habit,
she was laid up in the infirmary, very ill. She had
haemorrhages, and terrible attacks of asthma when it
seemed as though she must stifle during the spasms.
On Thursday, October 25, 1866, between nine and
ten o'clock at night, the Bishop was informed that
Bernadette was dying, and that the Superior-General
of the Sisters of Nevers asked for permission to admit
her to profession. Mgr. Forcade came himself to
Saint Gildard, and found the patient gasping and near
her last agony. She could not speak. He pronounced
the formula of the vows at her bedside, and she
answered simply, *Amen*. The prelate spoke a few
edifying words to the novice and blessed her, feeling
sure that he would not see her again in this world.

More than once, Bernadette had felt herself
suddenly relieved after terrible attacks of her asthma
and she then reacted energetically, remained sitting

up in bed and, as her breathing became easier, recovered speech. It was what happened again on this occasion. Shortly after the Bishop's departure, she suddenly felt she was reviving, and addressing herself to the Mother-General, who was still at her bedside, extremely anxious, she declared with her usual spontaneity and candour: 'Mother, you have made me make my Profession because you thought I should die to-night; well, I shall not die to-night.' The Superior-General, Mother Josephine Imbert, was, so Mgr. Forcade tells us, 'one of the most accomplished and most capable religious whom Heaven had ever given to her Institute, but she dreaded the danger of pride for the favoured child of Lourdes to such a degree, that she treated her coldly, even harshly, and humiliated her on every possible occasion.'

So, instead of showing any joy and motherly kindness on seeing her daughter return to life, Mother Josephine said to her in a severe tone: 'What! You knew that you would not die to-night, and you did not say so! You are nothing but a little idiot! I declare that if you are not dead to-morrow morning I shall take off the black veil of the Professed, that you have just been given, and send you back to the noviciate with the simple novice's veil.' To which, peaceful and smiling, Bernadette replied: 'As you please, dear Mother.'

When we consider it, this grave occurrence which put Bernadette in danger of death, and called forth the Bishop's intervention, confronts us with two widely differing states of mind that cannot but astonish us. In the first place, the behaviour of the Mother Superior, Josephine Imbert, is strange enough. Bernadette had been ill for several days; she suddenly felt herself better but, doubtless, was not yet out of danger. Should not the Reverend Mother have let her heart speak, expressed her satisfaction, and encouraged the little novice who was so ill? It is true that, by way of explaining her manner of proceeding, they tell us that 'fearing the danger of pride for Bernadette, she treated her harshly and humiliated her on every occasion.' Undoubtedly there was considerable truth in this observation, but a priest, a director of conscience who has gained by experience a shrewd knowledge of souls, even the souls of religious, is always distrustful of the reasons given under such circumstances in order to justify their conduct. St. John of the Cross tells us, more than once, that in fervent religious we may find eminent qualities side by side with very serious imperfections. He also informs us that under the most spiritual, even the most mystical pretexts, which seem to canonize our ways of proceeding, there may lurk, unknown to ourselves, motives inspired by our human nature and our temperament.

This observation is far more important that we usually realize. From the single example here given, we may have no difficulty in believing that Mother Josephine Imbert treated Bernadette very harshly on the pretext of humbling her, but had she much difficulty in so doing, and did she gain much merit thereby? We may ask ourselves the question. In the Process of Canonization, we read this evidence, given by Mother Josephine Forestier: 'Mother Josephine Imbert hesitated rather a long time before receiving Bernadette, and, seemingly, she had to be begged to admit her. Mgr. Forcade was annoyed about it when he preached the retreat to our Sisters at Toulouse, at which Mother-General was present. Everything leads me to think that he had to insist upon her giving him a final answer.'

This information alone would incline us to ask ourselves the question: Did Mother Imbert like Bernadette? Sister Henry Fabre witnesses: 'I remember how Bernadette confided to me, whilst bending down over the umbrella she was mending in order to hide herself: " Mother Josephine! Oh, how I fear her ! " ' For the moment, we shall leave the question unanswered. Let us turn at once to the second state of mind, still more astonishing under the circumstances than that of the Mother-General— that of the little novice of twenty-two, only three months after her entry into the noviciate.

What self-possession ! What self-abjection ! What humility must we not sense in the simple, gentle reply given with a smile to the Superior, and under such trying conditions, by one who was considered merely a rough, uncultured peasant girl ! 'As you please, dear Mother.' We declare without an instant's hesitation that St. Teresa of the Child Jesus, even after years of religious life, would have been incapable of improving upon it.

For several years previously, Bernadette had been striving to practise before all else the fundamental virtue of humility. We have seen that Jeanne Védère, who was much older than her cousin, and entered the Cistercians, where she received the name of Sister Gertrude, stated in her evidence: " I do not believe that Bernadette ever knew either self-love or vanity.' This statement is certainly exaggerated. Nevertheless, one of the Sisters of the Lourdes hospice, who had once taught Bernadette, said much the same: ' That child is very humble; she likes to be hidden.'

From the day she entered the Mother-House of Nevers, Bernadette was fully determined to hide herself, to progress more and more in the virtue of humility. One of the religious who saw her arrive in the noviciate as a postulant, says: 'She entered with two companions, and to our great surprise, she differed in nothing from the other postulant, unless it were in her greater humility.' This effort to acquire the virtue which spiritual writers declare is the most fundamental of the religious life, was very clearly defined and deliberate in Bernadette's case. On her Clothing day, borrowing the words of the *Imitation*, she said to her sisters: 'I have come to be hidden. I want to be forgotten, to be esteemed as nought.' One day, when the novice mistress had particularly mortified her, Sister Marie-Bernard replied to a novice who asked whether she had not felt hurt: 'Oh no! Our mistress is right, for I have plenty of pride. At Lourdes, I was too much esteemed, but now that I am here I shall work to correct myself.' She took all the measures calculated to make her progress in this precious virtue.

When during the day she had yielded to a slight movement of impatience, she repaired her fault by publicly accusing herself of it in the evening. She made every effort to convince herself more and more that, if she had been chosen as an instrument by Our Lady of Lourdes, it was because of her utter insignificance. If she were asked for prayers, she would answer: 'Yes, I will pray for you, but pray also for me, for I am very proud.' She often repeated in the parlour (these are her words): 'Our Lady made use of me as one does of a pebble or a broom. The broom is used to remove the dust. When you have finished your work, you put it behind the door, and it stays there. I am like that.' Canon Perreau, who knew her well, declares: 'She had declared a war to the death on her pride. She used to repeat as a prayer: "The love of our Lord will be the knife to cut and do away with the tree of pride and its evil roots.   The more I abase myself, the higher I shall raise myself in the Heart of Jesus." '

Let us anticipate the future from now, and not be astonished that during the Process of Canonization witnesses whose authority stands very high, such as Mother Josephine Forestier, should have attested: ' Humility was Sister Marie-Bernard's dominant virtue.'   Another, Sister Martha Durais, who had enjoyed her friendship and known her intimately, tells us: ' It seems to me that the Venerable Servant of God had attained to the summit of humility when I knew her.   She encouraged her companions to practise humility by her example and by her words.   Several times, she said to me: " This act of humility, we must do it." '

Three months after her Clothing, when she had just received the Last Sacraments, and at the moment when she was least expecting it was so harshly treated by the Superior-General, Bernadette had certainly not yet attained to the summit of sanctity; but she was advancing by giant strides in that virtue which is the essential characteristic of the way of spiritual childhood.

CHAPTER VII

PRAYER AND MEDITATION OF SISTER
MARIE-BERNARD

AS we have seen, on arriving at Nevers and entering the noviciate, Bernadette set herself from the first to keep the rule strictly, albeit without excessive rigour. She was in fact led by the Holy Spirit, and attached less importance to the letter of the law than to the spirit that gives it life. We have also seen that she found strength by striving to her utmost after an ever-deepening humility. There is another highly important primordial means of which we have not spoken, and to which Bernadette constantly had recourse : we mean prayer under all its forms.

When she was a child, the form of prayer most familiar to her had been the rosary. It was almost the only devotion she knew. It is true that when she had made progress in the knowledge of her religion she made use of other forms of prayer, but she always returned to the rosary, as the simplest and easiest way of going to God by way of Mary. Indeed, she had an exceptional facility for recollecting herself in prayer. ' Even as a child,' we are told, ' she prayed with great recollection. The church roof might have fallen before Bernadette would have turned her head.' This faculty of absorption which, without her realizing it, rendered her so fitted for contemplative prayer, edified her companions very greatly. ' I profited by every occasion of seeing her,' states Sister Irene Garnier, ' for I wished to gaze at those eyes that had seen the Blessed Virgin. As soon as she saw that anyone was looking at her, she would lower her eyes. . . . I saw her kneeling in the chapel before a statue of our Lady, saying her rosary in a deeply recollected manner, motionless and without any distraction.'

The religious who knew her are unanimous in stressing this incomparable devotion to the rosary. Sister Bernard Dalias attested: 'I shall never forget the expression of fervour which she put into the recitation of the rosary. For us all, she was an example which we would have wished to imitate.' The admiration of this witness is all the more valuable in that she is not at all suspect of *parti pris*. The fact is that when she arrived at Nevers as a postulant Sister Dalias had shown a desire to see Bernadette. She expected to be introduced to an imposing personage. When Bernadette, by far the smallest in the noviciate, came on the scene, very simple, quite natural, showing no signs whatever of the great recollection that always reigned in the depths of her soul, Mlle. Dalias could not help exclaiming too bluntly: '*That* is Bernadette!' Sister Marie-Bernard held out her hand and answered with a charming smile, for she was really enjoying the other's surprise, 'Yes, Mademoiselle, Bernadette is only *that!*' Sister Bernard watched her closely at prayer, and soon recognized that there were mysterious and incomparable depths of piety hidden in Bernadette. 'The sight of Bernadette at prayer made an indefinable impression upon me,' says another. The nun who beyond question knew her best and most intimately, Mother Eleanor Cassagnes, testifies: 'She used to recite the rosary with angelic piety. She always had it in her hand when going through the cloisters. As the novices used to say: "It encouraged us to do likewise."'

Bernadette did not say her rosary only during the day. 'During her long, sleepless nights,' we are assured by the chaplain, who had learnt the fact from the Saint, 'she used to say her rosary.' This last testimony raises a question not clearly answered hitherto. Did Bernadette say the rosary, properly speaking? Did she sometimes meditate on the mysteries? For we know that this meditation is necessary in order that the prayers recited may be called 'the rosary.' Although we have not absolutely precise information on this point, there seems no doubt about the matter. 'In her prayer,' we are told, 'she did not give herself up to lofty considerations, but was content to contemplate our Lord in His different mysteries, and to draw practical conclusions from them for her own guidance.' And it is immediately added: 'Among vocal prayers, she preferred the rosary.'

Undoubtedly, Bernadette was in the habit of meditating upon the mysteries, especially those of the Passion, but in a contemplative rather than in a discursive manner. She beheld them, so to speak, in a single glance with the eyes of her soul, and that predisposed her, almost necessarily, to recite the rosary formally when in community they recalled the corresponding mystery at each decade, or when she recalled it herself. 'The Venerable Servant of God,' attests Sister Casimir Callery, 'meditated upon the mysteries. One day, I owned to her that I could not pray. She replied confidentially: " Go in spirit to the Garden of Gethsemane, or to the foot of the Cross, and stay there. Our Lord will speak to you and you will listen." ' Once such a habit of silently contemplating the mysteries of the Passion and the Crucifixion has been acquired, it is impossible to say the decades of the rosary corresponding to these mysteries without saying the rosary, as properly understood.

Devotion to the rosary leads us, generally speaking, to meditation. Did Sister Marie-Bernard know how to meditate? We reply that the truth was that she practised rather affective prayer than what is strictly called meditation. When we consult the Process of Canonization, however, and when we study attentively the private notebook kept by Bernadette, in which she took note of the instructions during retreat, we see from the evidence that she was far from being incapable of meditation. On this subject, writers usually rely upon a reply made by her at Lourdes. The Sister responsible for training her said: 'At your age, you ought to meditate a little.' Bernadette answered: 'I! I don't know how to meditate.' She was then very ignorant. Indeed, it was during the period of the apparitions, but since then she had learnt to read, and had made great progress. Mother Bordenave states, in fact: 'According to the evidence of the Sisters at Lourdes, her progress in her studies was surprising.'

Once for all, we must rid ourselves, and that energetically, of the over-simplifying and too widespread prejudice, to-day prevalent almost everywhere, that Bernadette was an absolute ignoramus and of a rather low standard of mentality. Indeed, unless we do reject this untenable prejudice we shall find it impossible to understand her contemplation and mystical life. Undoubtedly, from the point of view of general instruction she was inferior to many of her companions, but she was very superior to them as regards judgement and understanding. 'She understood nothing of arithmetic,' testifies Sister Josepha Caldeiron, 'and she had received little education, although she was naturally very intelligent.' From

her relations with her cousin, Jeanne Védère, we
have learnt already that in spiritual matters her
judgement was very good; she had counselled the
latter as a thoroughly enlightened spiritual director
would have done. In the obituary notice of Sister
Marie-Bernard, Mgr. Forcade, who had known her
well, attests that she was endowed with intelligence
above the average. 'Having entered the noviciate
very ignorant, she there made such rapid progress in
her studies as to prove sufficiently that she possessed
abilities beyond the average. She was also what is
known as quick-witted, and her apt retorts and
sallies when persons tired her out with indiscreet
questions could leave no doubt on this point. This
quality even sparkled in her eyes, which were of an
indefinable clearness and beauty.'

In the best sense of the word, Sister Marie-Bernard
was curious about spiritual truth. An experienced
director, well acquainted with religious communities,
would make no mistake. Rarely do we find, especially among women who have not gone in for higher
studies, subjects whose minds are so open to instruction as was that of Bernadette. 'She loved spiritual
reading,' we are told, 'and made notes so that she
might know more about God.' How few are the
religious women absorbed in active works who do as
much ! It is often far from easy to persuade them
to devote a quarter of an hour to spiritual reading, and
if they recognize its utility in theory, in practice they
do nothing about it. Here we have a tangible proof
of Bernadette's aptitude and taste for the highest
spiritual truths. She had procured for herself a
small, private notebook, to which she consigned the
thoughts she had gathered in the course of sermons and
reading. This book contains also her own reflections
which, notwithstanding some spelling mistakes, are

not the least remarkable portion of its contents.   Although it is very regrettable that she has not expressed her own thought more at length and during the whole course of her religious life, what remains to us is amply sufficient to inform and edify us with respect to the interior work that was being accomplished both in her understanding and in her soul. The notes she takes during a retreat will even astonish us if, misled by the popular opinion, we are expecting to meet with an ignorant shepherdess.   Would we think, for example, that it is a choir nun or an uncultured lay sister who has been able to note down the following passage in a conference: ' *Look at St. John the Baptist at the Jordan; how austere and rigorous he is!   It is not yet Jesus, but how he is preparing the way for him!   How he urges men to contrition by penance!   How he announces Jesus!   How he leads men to Jesus!   How he effaces himself before Jesus!* Debes a te baptizari. *He consents only from humility, from obedience.*   Sic nos decet implere omnem justitiam, *Jesus said.*

Omnem: 1. as Saviour, by expiating.
　　　　2. as sinner: since He represents them in humbling Himself.
　　　　3. as the just: in purifying Himself yet more.' [1]

It goes without saying that Sister Marie-Bernard re-read her notebook, and meditated upon the passages which she had carefully copied in her fine

---

[1] We cite only this characteristic passage, which is found on p. 25 of the private notebook, but which will say much to preachers of retreats. The latter indeed know from experience that few or no nuns who have not received a secondary education are capable of summarizing the principal thoughts of an eloquent discourse.   Moreover, these notes are accompanied by reflections and applications that are distinctly personal.

writing. She loved to make her mental prayer with the community, and all the witnesses vie with one another in informing us how she used to lower her veil in order the better to hide herself; it was, she said, her little chapel. The Abbé Febvre, chaplain to the community, has written: ' She had that taste for divine things. As soon as I spoke to her about God, she became very attentive, but her attention was out of the common. Sometimes, I went to give her a resumé of the instruction given to the community when illness had prevented her from being present. She was extremely grateful. "Thank you," she would say; "if you knew how I regret not being able to be present at the instructions!"' No one who closely studies Bernadette, the nun, can have any doubt that hers was a soul eager for spiritual and mystical truths. She was instinctively orientated towards God.

Without proceeding according to a strict method, Sister Marie-Bernard neglected no means of obtaining instruction and pondering over it. She did not abandon herself exclusively and prematurely to a purely passive and contemplative form of prayer; at first, and especially during her noviciate, she applied herself to meditation. In the infirmary, she was always very deeply recollected. Thence she began, following the advice of the founder, Dom de Laveyne, to betake herself to a very simple form of meditation, in which the mysteries are considered by a simple look, ' whilst honouring them with humility until it please God to give us His light.' [1]

Throughout her year of noviciate, although she doubtless practised unawares this method of meditation, which the founder declared ' is very easy; seeing that it is very easy to humble ourselves before

---

[1] *Vie de Dom de Laveyne*, par la Mère Bordenave, p. 126.

God whilst begging Him to give us His light, as a poor man begs,' Sister Marie-Bernard endeavoured, and that rightly, to walk by the ordinary way as far as she could, and meditate.   She also greatly appreciated the instructions of her novice mistress, who was a zealous religious and possessed of a superior and cultured mind.

Some months after her entrance into the Mother-House, Bernadette received some bad news.   Her mother, worn out by family duties, and also much affected by the departure of her elder daughter, to whom she was specially devoted, gently passed away at Lourdes on December 8, 1866, the feast of the Immaculate Conception. On hearing of her death, Sister Marie-Bernard was so painfully affected that she fainted. At once they lavished upon her all the attentions usual under such circumstances.   When she came round, the novice reacted bravely and said: ' My God, Thou hast willed it.   May Thy holy Name be praised ! '   Here, in this scene, we have Bernadette portrayed completely; with her almost excessive sensitiveness and also with her amazing faculty for moral recovery.

All through her noviciate year, particularly during the last six months, she was especially tried by Mother Marie-Thérèse Vauzou, the mistress of novices.   All the witnesses without exception are at one in recognizing that the latter profited by every occasion to humiliate her. Sister Marie-Bernard endured this hard period of probation generously and humbly, and, by means of vocal and mental prayer, was led to seek increasingly, in union with God, the strength that was so constantly necessary to her.   She was also tried very often by Mother Josephine Imbert, the Superior-General.   Coming out from an instruction with a fellow novice, the two girls went to the infirmary to receive some attention, and met Mother Josephine Imbert, who treated them as good for nothing. Bernadette's companion, very sensitive to this reproach, burst into tears, but Bernadette remarked: ' Don't cry. We shall have plenty more of this ! ' She was far from mistaken, at least as regards herself. On returning from a journey, the Superior-General kissed all the novices, addressing some kind word to each of them; she embraced Bernadette without uttering a word. This little mark of coldness, which was noticed by every-one, might seem of small importance, but it had more than one might think in a religious community. When actions of this kind, apparently insignificant and imperceptible, are renewed on every occasion they become for a cloistered nun, for in consequence of her malady Bernadette was such, a heavy trial. Referring to this subject, St. Teresa of the Child Jesus said: 'I love them: these pin-pricks.' When Sister Marie-Bernard was reprimanded or underwent some humiliation, Sister Marcelline Durand relates how she would say: 'I have just received a sweet ! ' 'What sort of one?' asked the Sister. 'Oh, that is my business.' Those who are to become saints enter from the first on the same way of suffering. One of her fellow novices expressed the general opinion in this sentence, which is cited to-day by all the Saint's biographers: 'It is well not to be Bernadette ! '

During her noviciate, Sister Marie-Bernard had not been exempt from physical suffering. She spent more than a week in the infirmary, and one of her companions said to her: ' You are suffering much, are you not?' Bernadette, who had retained her outspokenness, replied: 'Oh, what would you have? Our Lady told me that I should not be happy in this world.' They admired her courage and patience, yet the novice was very sensitive and, above all, when she was ill, the slightest unpleasantness tried her patience. ' Her expression, which was extremely mobile,' we are told, ' sometimes revealed the violence she was exercising upon herself. She was quickly mistress of herself and lent herself to what was required of her with a good grace.'

' One day,' relates Sister Vincent Garros, who had been Bernadette's friend from her childhood, ' I told her I had brought all sorts of things for her from Lourdes; chocolate, pictures and statues, and that I had delivered all to the mistress of novices. Bernadette thus answered me: " Well, my poor dear, I shall never see any of it ! " ' Sister Vincent Garros had also shown her some photographs of the grotto and of herself. The novice mistress entered the infirmary at that moment, noticed the photographs, and said: ' Above all, do not show them to Bernadette.' Sister Vincent told the latter of the incident and Bernadette replied: ' The prohibition has come too late,' and began to laugh.

We can see that Sister Marie-Bernard did not attach undue importance to these secondary incidents. After dinner one day when she arrived at the infirmary earlier than usual, she was asked the reason and answered: ' I was politely asked to retire; no doubt because they were going to speak of Lourdes and show photographs.' Her noviciate year passed thus. The opinion of her novice mistress, Mother Marie-Thérèse Vauzou, set down in a private notebook, though severe, nevertheless mentions some essential virtues: ' *Character inflexible. Over-sensitive. Modest, pious, thorough. She has a sense of order.*'

In a few words, despite the noteworthy reserve at the beginning, it was a favourable report given by the novice mistress, and guaranteed admission to

Profession. Sister Marie-Bernard pronounced her vows, with her companions, on October 30, 1867. ' I have a vivid recollection,' says Sister Dalias, ' of the voice of Sister Marie-Bernard at the moment when she pronounced her vows. Her tone was firm and quiet, without any affectation. In the tribune, the singers were moved and held their breath in order to listen better.' The religious ceremony in the chapel had its sequel in the large common room of the noviciate.

The Bishop entered, gave a crucifix, a book of the Constitutions, and a letter of obedience or assignation to each of the newly professed, as she came and presented herself before him at the summons of the novice mistress.

Mgr. Forcade, Bishop of Nevers, has described this scene precisely and so vividly that we need only summarize his account. On the day of Sister Marie-Bernard's Profession, she alone was not called forward, and for her alone no letter of obedience had been prepared. It is well known how, once their noviciate is ended, novices impatiently await the obedience which will destine them to such or such an employment in such or such a house of their order. They talk of it among themselves. No doubt, Bernadette expected to be sent to some community similar to that at Lourdes, in which she would be able to render some service. Henri Bremond has very rightly remarked that for devout and contemplative souls who are suffering from their environment, such departure means a deliverance. The Mother-General, on the contrary, had decided that Sister Marie-Bernard's place was at the Mother-House, and that it was there that she should live and die. This decision was indisputably very wise and inspired by Providence. As a rule, it was a favour to be assigned to the Mother-House, but they were going to make Bernadette pay dearly for it.   All the novices who had just pronounced their vows were called in turn, but Sister Marie-Bernard waited in vain for her name to be called out.   She was not called.   Forewarned, the Bishop then asked: ' Why has Sister Marie-Bernard not been called, and why has no letter of obedience been given me for her?'   The Superior-General rose and, assuming her grand manner, replied: ' My Lord, it is not possible to assign her an obedience.'   And she added: ' She is a little dolt and good for nothing.'   And she resumed her seat.

Here we leave Mgr. Forcade to speak:

' " Sister Marie-Bernard, come here."   She came and knelt at my feet.

' " So you are good for nothing ? "

' " Mother-General is right.   It is quite true."

' " But then, my poor child, what are we to do with you, and what was the use of your entering the Congregation ? "

' " That was exactly what I said to Your Lordship at Lourdes, and you answered me that it did not matter."

' I was not in the least expecting that response,' says the Bishop, ' and frankly I did not know what to say.   Mother Josephine came to my aid and again rose to her feet.

' " If Your Lordship is willing, we can keep her at the Mother-House, out of charity, and find something for her to do in the infirmary.   As she is nearly always ill, it will just suit her.   To begin with, she will simply be employed in cleaning; then, perhaps, later on, we might set her to preparing herbal drinks, if we can ever find any means of teaching her."   Certainly, there was nothing there likely to turn Bernadette's head.'

The latter's fellow religious tell us that she generously bore this public humiliation, but not without suffering under it. The reader will have noticed that the Bishop did not foresee the solution which would put an end to the paltry farce. In particular, he did not know that they were reserving for her the office of assistant infirmarian.

This incident arouses in the psychologist reflections which it is impossible for him to suppress. In her biography, *The Humble Saint Bernadette*, Colette Yver has justly observed, although in a summary manner: ' It is the humiliation that is wounding, deliberately thought out, willed, that pride finds it hardest not to resent. It is easier to remain humble under praise than under insult.' We admit that we were somewhat surprised to meet with this remark, worthy of an experienced confessor and director, in a secular writer, but it calls for some further development.

Hello wrote that one who possesses an unrecognized capacity is never more aware of it than when those who surround him are thus mistaken in his regard. It is the same in the case of a virtue. A soul that knows that it possesses a wisdom and capacity above the average, which cannot doubt as to such despite all its humility—for there are truths, and an intimate knowledge of one's own capability that are self-evident—feels itself the more strongly urged to assert its gifts in that its companions deny, or affect to deny them.

Bernadette, let us stress the fact, replies to her Bishop after the unflattering estimate of the Mother-General, that she is, indeed, useless; that that was precisely what she had said at Lourdes. That Sister Marie-Bernard would have been incapable of regularly fulfilling the duties of an office of importance was true; for that she had not sufficient health;

but she had always cherished a sort of cultus for the truth. She was able to declare to her companions that she had never told a lie; hers was a noble and loyal soul. Consequently, she accepted without difficulty the undeniable element of truth contained in the Superior's speech. But that she was 'a simpleton,' a 'dolt,' as Mother Josephine Imbert had already told her when she had pronounced her vows on a sick bed, and repeated when she had made them publicly, was quite contrary to the truth. The fact was that, if there was one thing which Bernadette was not, it was a simpleton. On the contrary, as we have been frequently told, she was endowed with precociously good sense and sound judgement, and her faculties were harmoniously balanced. On the other hand, it is true that she was very weak at arithmetic and spelling, but very capable at household duties, and at needlework. When the Superior told the Bishop: 'We might be able later on to set her to preparing herbal drinks, if we can ever find any means of teaching her,' Bernadette, despite all her modesty, could not but have thought immediately that she could make *tisane* as well as, and better than, her companions. The humiliation inflicted, without much care for exactitude or proportion, upon Sister Marie-Bernard on her Profession day must necessarily have given rise within her to many and varied reflections and to temptations to rebellion. Everything within her cried out that this was not true, that her Superior and Sisters would be very surprised when she set to work. Given her quick temperament, sickly and highly strung as she was, it must have needed heroic virtue under the circumstances to resist the secret temptations originating, as she said, 'from the human " I," ' and encouraged also by the devil who, according to St. John of the

Cross, St. Teresa, the Curé d'Ars, and the leading lights of mystical theology, never fails to exercise his deleterious influence in the weaker parts of man's nature, above all in the cases of those whom he feels are predestined to sanctity and to a mission of general atonement. It is clearly in this sense that we must explain the statement already mentioned of the Abbé Febvre, the chaplain. 'I have sometimes thought that these movements of ill-humour were partly the effect of an uncommon diabolic action. The evil spirit was vanquished in the end, for Bernadette soon humbled herself.'

Sister Marie-Bernard will constantly accuse herself of being proud. In fact, she was much less so than another; but being aware of hidden capability beneath the outward appearances of ignorance and incapacity, and of a providential mission to be fulfilled, she often felt urged to rebel under the remarks and treatment that wounded her. This was one of the temptations against which she had to struggle until her dying day.

CHAPTER VIII

Sister Marie-Bernard as Assistant Infirmarian and Second Sacristan

BERNADETTE had made her religious Profession on October 30, 1867, as we have seen; she had then been appointed Assistant Infirmarian at the Mother-House. She remained in this office until 1874, that is, for seven years. She was, however, frequently ill and obliged to stay in bed in the infirmary. All the religious who saw her at work agree in attesting that she carried out her duties with thoughtful and intelligent charity. Sister Bernard Dalias tells us: ' It was a joy for the sick to be nursed by Sister Marie-Bernard.' Mother Josephine Forestier, having returned to the Mother-House very ill, states: ' They put me into the infirmary with Sister Marie-Bernard. It was she who nursed me with infinitely delicate care.'

Although second infirmarian, Sister Marie-Bernard was not only extremely kind and gentle, but knew how to see that the doctor's orders were obeyed to the letter, as well as the regimen he prescribed. One novice, as a result of one of those keenly felt trials which seem insignificant to the general reader but profoundly affect religious, had two attacks of high fever, and a third was feared. Guessing the cause of the trouble, the novice mistress came to comfort her. The intelligent care which Sister Marie-Bernard bestowed upon the patient brought about an almost sudden improvement. In the morning, without permission, the novice rose, went to hear Mass, and towards eight o'clock returned to the infirmary. A companion told her that Sister Marie-Bernard was displeased at her leaving her bed without permission, and the patient went to look for the latter and explained her reasons for so doing. 'Sister Marie-Bernard,' she says, 'spoke to me in such a tone of religious obedience, which is as binding in the infirmary as in the noviciate, that I asked her, "What ought I to do?" "Return to bed." It cost me something, but Sister Marie-Bernard had so convinced me that I gave in to her wish at once.' We may see that the assistant exercised real authority, and never temporized where duty was involved. It is sufficiently astonishing that a religious so small in stature, so retiring, and passing for an ignoramus, should have had such prestige. 'There was,' says Sister Cécile Pagès, 'an old nun who had no longer her mental faculties. As her room was next to the infirmary, she often caused a noise. Only Sister Marie-Bernard could make her see reason. This religious sometimes flattered Bernadette in order to make the latter yield to her caprices, but the infirmarian remained firm. Sister Marie-Bernard discovered how to make herself loved and obeyed.'

Here we find again Bernadette, the elder daughter of the Subirous, who could take her parents' place and rule her brothers and sister. A sick postulant, whom she had told to remain in bed and keep her shoulders well covered, took up her *Manual of the Children of Mary*, and began to say the Little Office of Our Lady. Catching her in the act, Sister Marie-Bernard exclaimed: 'There you have a fervour made up of disobedience.' She took possession of the book, which the postulant never saw again. As we can see, when it was necessary Bernadette took a strong line with her patients. She was, moreover, herself very courageous, and conscientiously carried out the duties of her office despite her weakness. ' In her work as assistant infirmarian,' we are told, ' Sister Marie-Bernard, when not ill, showed herself very skilful. As soon as she was able to get up, she went to her work for she was not afraid of suffering. I have seen her suffering from oppression, but going about just the same.'   One day, she had to prepare for burial a former Superior who had just died.   They were laying out the dead and Sister Marie-Bernard said to Sister Vincent Garros : ' Come and help me.' The Sister hesitated, owing to her repugnance for the task, and refused.   Bernadette retorted : ' You are a coward ! You will never make a Sister of Charity.'

Not only did Sister Marie-Bernard nurse her patients with unlimited devotion and a delicate thoughtfulness, but notwithstanding her own weariness, her trials and interior sadness, she was always kind and smiling.   Knowing how sick people need to breathe a cheerful atmosphere as flowers need the sun's rays, ' she tried to cheer up her patients with interesting stories, in which the note of piety was ever dominant, so that they forgot their troubles.' Moreover, she prayed especially fervently for those who were suffering most ; she appealed to Our Lady of Lourdes, who heard her prayers.   One novice was enduring such pain that it forced her to cry out. Sister Marie-Bernard said to a companion : ' We are going to give her some Lourdes water to relieve her ; come, kneel beside me and, above all, let us be fervent.'   Almost on the instant, the novice ceased to suffer.

A well-known incident from another source comes to confirm the evidence of the religious concerning the capabilities of Bernadette as an infirmarian. Doctor Voisin, a specialist at the Salpêtrière, when developing his theories with respect to hallucination which, according to him, always ended in insanity, cited as a proven example Bernadette. He stated that she ' was confined as a lunatic in the convent of the Ursulines of Nevers.' So rash and unfounded an assurance astonishes us to-day. The professor had not made any investigations, nevertheless the newspapers published his statement. The Bishop of Nevers, Mgr. Forcade, replied through the press:

' I have the honour to declare:

' 1. That Sister Marie-Bernard has never set foot in the Ursuline convent of Nevers.
' 2. That it is true that she resides at Nevers, in the Mother-House of the *Sisters of Charity and Christian Instruction ;* that she has entered and remained there as perfectly freely as any other Sister.
' 2. That far from being a lunatic, she is an unusually sensible person, and imperturbably calm.

' Furthermore, I venture to invite the aforesaid distinguished professor, whose name I do not remember, to come in person and verify the truth of these three statements. . . . I will undertake myself to bring him into immediate contact with Sister Marie-Bernard, and in order that he may not conceive any doubt as to her identity, I will request the Prefect of the Republic to be kind enough to introduce her to him. He will then be free to look at her, question her, even to pester her, as long as he may see fit.'

Naturally, Professor Voisin remained at the Salpêtrière and took good care not to reply. The fact is instructive. It teaches us to distrust the risky and unjustified hypotheses that, often enough, specialists of the highest repute will launch forth, lightly and without any foundation, when religious matters are in question. The theories which explained the visions of St. Teresa the Great and other saints on the grounds of hysteria were hardly more serious.

After the publication of Doctor Voisin's lecture, Doctor Damoiseau, President of the Medical Board of the Department of the Orne, wrote to Doctor Robert Saint-Cyr, President of that of the Nièvre, asking him to give him very precise details as to the mental condition of Bernadette. The last-named physician replied as follows:

' My dear colleague,
    ' You could not have applied to a better source in order to have the information you desire concerning the young Lourdes girl, to-day Sister Marie-Bernard. As the doctor of her community, during a long period I have attended this young nun, whose very delicate health caused us great anxiety. Her condition has now improved, and from being my patient, she has become my nurse and carries out her duties to perfection.

' Small, frail in appearance, she is twenty-seven years of age. Her temperament is calm and gentle; she nurses her patients very intelligently and omits nothing that I have ordered. Hence she has great authority, and for my part enjoys my entire confidence.

' You see, my dear colleague, that this young Sister is very far from being insane. I will say more: her calm, simple, quiet temperament does not predispose her, in the least degree, to the danger of failing in this respect.'

Sister Marie-Bernard was not only a devoted and capable infirmarian, but being often very ill herself, she set a fine example of obedience, resignation and courage to all the religious who passed through the infirmary.   ' In October, 1869,' deposes Sister Pagès, ' Sister Marie-Bernard was confined to bed, was coughing up blood by basinsful, and had two blisters on her back.   She was not tender of herself, and when I was dressing the sore places, said: " You can pull, my dear. I am as hard to kill as a cat!"'   The heroic courage of which she gave proof recalls that shown by St. Teresa òf the Child Jesus during her last illness, when, betaking herself to the chapel to say the Office, she said to herself: ' If I die, they will see it.'   Bernadette, likewise, went to the chapel, notwithstanding her exhaustion.   ' It happened,' relates Canon Perreau, ' that she fainted, collapsing on the altar steps.   Then she accused herself, saying: "Oh, dear Sisters, how scandalized you must be at my want of courage!"'   Far from seeing any want of courage there, they rightly considered that she was giving proof of supernatural strength.

And this supernatural strength she drew from all the sources of grace, by means of her favourite devotions and, above all, by mental prayer. We have shown already that from her noviciate she had especially practised the devotion of the rosary and meditation.   Although, as we have also shown, discursive meditation had never been separated from affective prayer in Bernadette's case, the more she progressed in the religious life the more she clung to mental prayer properly so called.   As we have said, she was infirmarian until 1874. She had not many more years to live. A statement of Canon Perreau is very significant: ' Very regular in making her prayer with the community, at the close of her life, distressed at

being no longer able to follow the subject of meditation, she consulted the chaplain, who said to her:
" Console yourself.   Make your prayer at the foot of
the Cross, by hiding yourself in our Lord's wounds."
The Venerable Servant of God replied: " Oh, how
those words do me good ! " '

She was always intensely recollected, and so her
life came to be lived in a state of prayer, which is,
we hold, what characterizes the mystics.   Without
keeping their eyes always cast down, without over-
much restraint, by avoiding all dissipation they are
accustomed, nevertheless, to maintain themselves
always in a disposition bordering upon prayer.
When Bernadette was at recreation, she was expansive,
cheerful, and ready to joke, but the moment the
bell rang her Sisters were both astonished and
edified to see how she promptly entered again
into a deep recollection.   It is important to notice,
however, that Bernadette highly valued this habit
of recollection, and that she had worked hard to
acquire it.

' She prepared herself for her mental prayer,' we
are told, ' by an interior recollection which was for
some time the object of her particular examen.   She
had reached a stage when during a week she had to
register only two failures on this point.   A postulant
met her in the cloister, and Sister Marie-Bernard,
who knew her well, and who, owing to her age in
religion, already enjoyed a certain authority, took
her aside and said to her: " Mademoiselle Marie,
you are not recollected but dissipated.   Why are
you always laughing in the refectory?   It is wrong." '
This unstrained but energetic watchfulness over oneself is the most necessary and often the most neglected
part of our preparation for prayer.   Bernadette knew
it, and that was why she did not hesitate to reprove

in the cloister one of her younger Sisters. ' She always kept her mind uplifted to God. In her words, in conversation, she often spoke of God. I know this from my personal knowledge,' affirms a witness, ' having verified it myself when talking to her.'

Like all mystical souls closely united to our Lord, who suffer both in body and soul, Sister Marie-Bernard had a very special devotion to the Passion. ' The Sorrowful Mysteries were those upon which she dwelt most often.' According to Sister Philippine Moliniéri, when she was in the infirmary, no matter how serious her sufferings might be, she was always seen to sit up in bed at the time of mental prayer, and she then appeared wholly absorbed in the duty she was fulfilling. When she felt a little less ill, and could leave her bed, whether in the cloisters or the chapel, she showed ' an attitude of piety and recollection such as I did not notice in the same degree in the cases of the other religious.'

She had taken up the practice of making the Stations of the Cross, and this she never omitted as long as she was able to fulfil it. ' Unless prevented by her health, she made them every day in the community chapel, kneeling on the tiles.' This daily devotion to which she, who was making great strides in the path of holiness, devoted herself, imprinted upon her mind the principal scenes of the Passion. The fourteen Stations, which she had so often contemplated, had become familiar and were for her as so many ' dwellings ' in which she could take refuge during the days and nights which she spent in bed.

Sister Marie-Bernard's devotion to the Passion of our Lord prepared her the better to understand the Mass, and to unite herself to Him by spiritual and sacramental Communion. 'She had a very great devotion to the Holy Sacrifice of the Mass,' we are told. 'Amidst her sharpest sufferings and her sleepless nights, her joy lay in uniting herself to the Holy Sacrifice.' So, again, by this means, she lived in constant contact with our Lord. She was also very exact in never omitting her visit to the Blessed Sacrament. When ill, and no longer able to walk, 'she had herself wheeled to the chapel by her sisters, who were glad to render her this service. Sometimes, she made this visit hidden in a corner of the tribune adjoining the infirmary.' We can easily imagine Bernadette, quite small as she was, hidden in the shadow, surrendering herself to the love for her Lord in the Host that was consuming her. By an almost necessary association of ideas, our thoughts turn to Sister Elizabeth of the Trinity, who also loved to conceal herself in the shadow before the Blessed Sacrament, in order to satisfy her devotion to the Eucharistic Lord; the saints resemble one another in their behaviour. So buried in her recollection was Bernadette in the tribune, that nothing could disturb her. The children belonging to the choir, who were taken there on the occasion of a ceremony, or for choir practice, would come in without her noticing them. 'She remained as motionless as a statue.'

The days on which she was allowed to receive Holy Communion were days of strengthening for her. 'I have seen her in the infirmary,' states Sister Stanislaus Pascal, 'preparing for Holy Communion with the fervour of a seraph. There she was, kneeling before a statue of our Blessed Lady, gazing upon her with one of those expressive looks that recalled the time of the apparitions.' Her face was lit up and radiant. When she was ill, the chaplain used to bring her Holy Communion. 'Sometimes,' he says, 'I was obliged to wait until an attack of asthma had passed in order to communicate her. Her look, fully recollected and yet lovingly turned towards the sacred Host, made a vivid impression upon me.'

Would one believe it? Yet nothing is more frequently found in the lives of the saints! She writes in her private notebook: 'Meditation is the preparation for Holy Communion. I make it so badly! Renew, strengthen the resolutions I have made upon this point.' As far as possible, Sister Marie-Bernard rose in the morning, although worn out, and went to receive the Eucharist in the chapel; sometimes she hesitated, but she would encourage herself by the examples of the most zealous servants of God; she knew from experience what an heroic effort is required for invalids who have suffered during sleepless nights to begin the day. 'One is so tired in the morning,' she writes in the precious little book. 'Remind myself of the temptation of Père Avila, when hesitating one day because of weariness, to continue on his way to go and say Mass. Our Lord appeared to him, and, showing him the wound in His heart, reminded him that weariness had not hindered Him from going to the top of Calvary. Courage! I also must know how to do violence to myself. After all, if I am tired, if I am exhausted, let me rest on the Heart of Jesus.'

Usually Bernadette was rewarded for the violence she did herself by interior consolations and the gift of tears. More favoured in this respect than was St. Teresa of the Child Jesus, she would not have to say, like the latter: 'There is no time when I find myself in greater aridity than during that of my thanksgiving.' 'Sitting near to her in the chapel,' attests Sister Philomena Girard, 'I often saw her shed tears

freely after Holy Communion.' Her recollection
became near to complete absorption. Really disconcerting accidents happened to her. ' One Christ-
mas night, she was so buried in her communing
with our Lord that everyone had left the chapel
without her having noticed them. She was nearly
shut in.'

In 1873, daily Communion was not yet practised
in religious communities. Bernadette longed to communicate very frequently, especially when she was
very ill and sorely tried on her bed of suffering.
' But they would not bring her Holy Communion
more often than to the Superior-General, who was
confined to her room.' She herself wrote on April 28,
1873, to her sister, Toinette-Marie :

' I hasten, dear Marie, to give you news of my
health. Here I am once more raised up, after having
been three months in bed. I was coughing blood
badly, and at the least movement it began again. I
had the happiness of receiving our Lord into my
poor, unworthy heart three times a week, all the time
I was ill. The cross became lighter, the sufferings
sweet, when I thought how I should have His visit,
and the great favour of possessing Him in my heart,
He who comes to suffer with those who suffer, to
weep with those who weep. Where can we find a
friend who knows how to sympathize, and at the
same time to ease our pains, like Jesus? It belongs
only to Him, to Jesus alone. Let us love Him and
cling to Him with our whole heart.'

This letter, addressed to her younger sister, which
we cannot suspect of having been dictated or corrected
by the Sisters of Nevers, undoubtedly confirms the
preceding evidence, and shows us to what a degree
the piety of Sister Marie-Bernard, and her prayer,

were Eucharistic. Truly, she lived in constant communion with the Blessed Sacrament and with the
Holy Sacrifice of which the celebration never ceases
at any instant somewhere in the world. She was
happy, especially at night, when she thought how, at
every moment, priests are consecrating the Host and
saying Mass.

After these essential devotions, the Holy Eucharist,
the Passion, the Stations of the Cross and the rosary,
Bernadette had still some private ones. ' Every day
I go in spirit to make my pilgrimage to the grotto of
Lourdes.' Closing her eyes, she endeavoured to see
again in imagination the features of Mary Immaculate.
' I do not see her again,' she said, ' if I have not been
good.' She meant to refer to her quick retorts, her
signs of impatience, her feelings of annoyance which,
when she was suffering physically and morally,
escaped her as first movements. These brusque outbursts, sometimes rather sudden and violent, which
disconcerted those around her and even led some
religious to doubt as to her holiness and her providential mission, were in reality only passing irrit-
ability, quickly enough repressed and caused by
nervous tension. Mother Josephine Forestier declared quite justly, during the Process of Canonization : ' Sister Marie-Bernard's impatience did not
arise from her rustic uncouthness but was due to her
constant invalid condition.' Bernadette, who reproached herself for her movements of anger as being
culpable imperfections, one day unwittingly exoner-
ated herself. The chaplain, the Abbé Febvre, had
been explaining in a sermon that one did not sin
unless there were a will to sin. At the next recreation, Sister Marie-Bernard said confidentially to one
of her sisters : ' Oh, I am so happy ! Did you hear
in our chaplain's sermon ? Unless we will to sin, we

9

do not sin. Well! I never remember having willed to sin.'

This statement is important. Those sharp speeches, frequent enough, which humiliated Bernadette and, if we are to believe M. Febvre, 'kept her heart detached from everything,' had in no way stained her baptismal innocence. Like St. Teresa of the Child Jesus, not only had Bernadette never committed a mortal sin, but not even serious, venial sins, premeditated or deliberate, with full knowledge. No doubt that was one of the reasons why the Immaculate Virgin chose her to expiate the faults of sinners who had sinned gravely. As to her chastity, she was and remained ever perfectly pure, with an innocence untroubled by the slightest temptation. 'I know from personal knowledge,' testifies Canon Perreau, ' that chastity, virginal purity, was the special attraction of the Venerable Servant of God. This purity shone resplendent in her to such a degree that those who spoke to her in private, as I did, were impressed by it. Whenever I conversed with her, I seemed to be in the presence of an angelic soul; it was that which showed itself in her gaze, full of innocence and purity. One day, a little girl walked out of the infirmary backwards, so as to lose nothing of the impression Bernadette had made upon her. She exercised an irresistible charm over little children.' She herself felt an attraction for the latter which rendered her exceptionally lovable. When the little servers came to bring some message, she gave them the sweetest smile and even added some little caressing action. She readily spoke to them about the grotto and Our Lady of Lourdes, and, silent person though she usually was, she would then find it hard to stop.

When, for the sake of charity, she was asked to

pay some visit which would ordinarily have been unwelcome to her, she lent herself to it with all good will. ' My mother having come to see me at Nevers,' writes a religious, ' I took her to Saint Gildard, in order to satisfy her desire to see Bernadette. I caught sight of the latter in the garden and went up to her, but as soon as she saw a stranger beside me she made off. I ended by rejoining her and said: " If your mother were here, I would receive her as graciously as I could." Seeing that she had hurt me, she hastily came up to my mother, greeted her cordially and was charming to her.' We can see that in order to defend herself from importunate visits and questions, Sister Marie-Bernard could be a hedgehog, as we may gather from the Abbé Febvre; but when she wished she could be extremely charming, and captivated her visitors in a few moments. The mother of the religious of whom we have just spoken said to her daughter, whom she had not seen for long years: ' I am very happy to have spent a short time with you, but I am happier still to have seen and kissed Bernadette.' Very courteous also from deference, Sister Marie-Bernard was, nevertheless, less gracious to bishops. Sometimes the younger Sisters went to spend the day at Coulanges, in a small country house near Nevers. Bernadette liked to sit near a little stream that flowed beside an alley of trees. She enjoyed the beauties of nature with the liberty of the children of God, as St. Francis of Assisi could with his brethren. ' It reminds me of Lourdes,' she would say. One afternoon, someone came to inform her that some bishops were waiting to see her and her sisters, but it goes without saying that it was for her that the prelates had put themselves out. ' These good bishops,' remarked Bernadette, with a spice of humour, ' would do much better to stay in their

dioceses than to demand to see us in the parlour.'
In her case, this sort of aversion for visits from
prelates was not accidental, as might be thought,
but constant. ' I must go to the parlour again;
if you knew what it costs me, above all if there are
bishops ! '

We shall excuse Bernadette if we remember to
what a degree, for more than ten years, she had been
harassed with visits of all kinds. Even during times
of retreat, or great ceremonies, the visiting Sisters,
who had come into the house, pestered her without
realizing it. Mother Henry Fabre confides to us:
' On one occasion, Bernadette came and said to me:
" There are too many people in the house. They
stare at me and try to see me, and it upsets me. Do
come and take a turn round the enclosure with me." '
The religious would point her out to their relatives
by her short stature. She was, indeed, the smallest
of them all, so that when the community walked in
double rank she was always placed first.

In 1874 Sister Marie-Bernard was relieved from
her office of infirmarian. The doctor rightly considered that the atmosphere of the infirmary was not
sufficiently healthy for her, and perhaps also, without
saying anything about it, he feared lest, afflicted with
advanced tuberculosis, Bernadette might be a dangerous source of infection to the sick whom she nursed.
She was then given charge of the chapel and the
vestments, as second sacristan, but she was to hold
this office for a short time only. The day was not
far distant, in fact, when she would be hardly anything more than an invalid. There was also another
drawback to this employment as sacristan. Necessarily obliged to be frequently in the chapel, she
found that visitors came to know this, and used to
come to see her. Meeting this seemingly quite

ordinary little nun, and unable to imagine that she could be the celebrated visionary, favoured with the apparitions at Lourdes, some of them would come forward and ask her in a whisper to go and find Bernadette, or to point her out to them. Sister Marie-Bernard would answer them with her most amiable smile, tinged, however, with a quite imperceptible expression of mischief, and with a slight nod disappear as though she were going to look for the celebrated religious, who, of course, kept the visitor waiting indefinitely. One day, in church, a lady who was better informed recognized her and kissed her skirt. At once Sister Marie-Bernard went and knocked on the door of the room of the Superior-General. ' Oh, Mother,' she implored, ' I beg of you, if I must endure such insults, to allow me never to come down to church, and remain always in a corner of the tribune.'

All these little incidents, which could doubtless be multiplied, give us a fair idea of the liberty of spirit in which Bernadette lived. She was one of the least formal saints who ever lived, yet none the less she dwelt continually in that abiding recollection that is so near to prayer, and which we have tried to describe. When she was very busy in the infirmary, the sacristy, or the chapel, she still prayed. Sister Martha Durais had heard her say: ' When I cannot make long prayers, I make up for it by ejaculatory ones.' She also turned to her favourite saints very familiarly. ' Faith,' said the Curé d'Ars, ' is when we pray to the saints as to friends.' Sister Marie-Bernard had a great devotion to St. Joseph. She liked to go and recollect herself in the beautiful chapel which was dedicated to him in the garden of the community, and often went there to make her mental prayer. She had the greatest confidence in the foster father of the Holy Family. One day in the infirmary, a Sister was suffering very severely. Bernadette said to her: ' I am going to pray to my father to relieve you.' As the other did not understand and showed surprise, Bernadette said: ' Oh, yes; you do not know that St. Joseph is my father,' and went to present her request. The religious drew her attention to the fact that she was praying to St. Joseph before a statue of Our Lady, but the Saint replied: ' That does not matter. They always understand in heaven. The saints are not jealous of one another.'

She had fostered a very special affection for St. John the Evangelist, because he had rested his head on the breast of our Lord, and was the divine Master's best-loved disciple. She had also a particular attraction towards St. Francis of Assisi, because of his simplicity, his love of suffering and of Jesus crucified. Because of this last trait, the year before she died, she had herself affiliated to the association of the Cord of St. Francis.[1]

When authors treat *ex-professo* of states of prayer, without knowing it they may convey an idea of the supernatural and mystical life that leads to its being considered exclusively under an aspect that is grave, complicated, and even slightly austere. In reality, although wholly immersed in prayer, the life of the

---

[1] Our Lord gave St. Francis of Assisi to St. Margaret Mary as her special guide. Marked with the sacred Stigmata, passionately in love with holy Poverty, desiring to know nothing but Jesus Christ and Him crucified, Francis had been on earth a living image of the Saviour of the world. Our Lord told St. Margaret Mary that it was as a pledge of His divine love that He was giving her such a protector to lead her through her trials and sufferings. (*Vie de Sainte Marguerite-Marie*, published by the monastery of Paray-le-Monial, p. 57.) St. Bernadette will also have St. Francis for a protector. These coincidences indicate to us in what genus of sanctity, so to speak, Bernadette is to be placed.

saints is very simple and very free from constraint. In spite of, or perhaps because of, her relative ignorance and want of intellectual culture, Bernadette was an intensely prayerful soul, a great mystic. During the last five years of her life, she had to carry out the greatest and noblest of offices : that of a victim called to expiate the faults of sinners.

CHAPTER IX

BERNADETTE BEGINS HER SUPERNATURAL VOCATION OF VICARIOUS SACRIFICE

BERNADETTE had heard from our Lady this exhortation, of which we have emphasized the primary importance: Penance! Penance! Penance! She had interpreted this divine warning by saying: 'I must first do penance for my own sins, and then for others.' She was devoted and divinely destined to the office of a victim. We have already pointed out that to be a pure victim to expiate the sins of men is a rare and very high vocation. Souls that are seriously aware of being such, must first have gone through the active and passive purifications which have corrected them of their own faults. That is why it is rare that those who have been converted after having committed many and very grave sins have any consciousness of being victims for others. Saints who were once such sinners may, no doubt, be victims, but they always fear lest they have not sufficiently expiated their own sins, the gravity of which they are apt to exaggerate. For this reason, generally speaking, and save for exceptions which are always possible and relatively many, souls that are clearly aware that they are suffering for their brethren are usually very pure and have never committed serious sins. We might cite as examples among others, St. Catherine of Siena, St. Teresa of the Child Jesus, and also Bernadette. We may even venture to say that Sister Marie-Bernard became very distinctly conscious of her vocation as an expiatory victim only during the last years of her life.

How was she to be a victim? How did she continue the Passion of Christ? How was she a martyr? The first answer to these queries is very easy. From her early youth, since the apparitions, she had scarcely ceased to suffer cruelly in her body, at least at frequently recurring intervals. At the moment when she was least expecting them, violent attacks of the asthma which never left her would choke her, and really cause suffocation, so that those around her then believed she was going to die. Several times she received the Last Sacraments. Tuberculosis was ravaging her frame, and making slow but inexorable progress. At the close of her life, her state of health became truly lamentable. ' Although often obliged to spend whole nights sitting on the edge of her bed, her feet on a chair, because she was suffering from oppression and had difficulty in breathing, suffocated with her cough and from the blood she vomited from time to time, I never heard her say: " I am suffering; I am tired," ' we are told in the Process. ' I said to her, " Poor Sister, you are suffering very much "; she replied: " I must. It is nothing." '

As was to be expected, her sufferings were aggravated by fresh complications due to the progress of the tuberculosis, and these increased up to her last day. ' During the last two years of her life,' we learn, ' a tumour had developed upon the right knee, which was followed by caries of the bone. Her whole body was one wound, so that during the last days she could not lie in bed and remained sitting in an armchair. She bore it all without complaint; she so loved her sufferings. One day, a Superior came to visit her and said: " What are you doing in bed, you lazy little thing?" She replied: "But I am doing my work. I must be a victim." She was aware that for her such was the divine plan.' So speaks Canon Perreau, who knew her personally.

Bernadette was right a thousand times in saying that she was doing her work in being ill, for the many and varied maladies held a great and absolutely essential part in her destiny as a victim. Asthma, haemorrhages, prolonged abscesses in the knee and in the ears, immobility, deafness, caries of the bones, an almost permanent state of insomnia that aggravated her often intolerable pains; such was her lot of bodily suffering, and well might she reply to the Sisters who pitied her: ' The Blessed Virgin told me that I should not be happy in this world.'

Considering the matter from the standpoint of Thomist philosophy, which emphasizes the close union between soul and body, we must take great account of this suffering state, and of the nervous tension which resulted from it, if we are to estimate rightly the moral trials which Bernadette had also to go through. Certain moral or spiritual sufferings may take their rise from the physical condition, others may be accidental, such as the failure of a friend, the death of a sister or a dearly-loved companion. These accidental trials, however, are felt in quite a different way by a person who is very much weakened and very ill, from that in which they are felt by another in good health. St. Teresa of the Child Jesus suffered until her death from serious temptations against faith, and these were much more trying to the Carmelite, who could no longer enjoy rest and sleep, than would have been the case in a nun who was more robust. Hence we must bear in mind that often Bernadette's body was one raw wound, that she was suffering without respite day and night, in order to understand in all its gravity what her heavy moral trial meant.

The question now arises: Did Bernadette endure, almost throughout her religious life, and until her death, a very heavy moral trial, that was in no way the result of her disease? There can be no doubt as to the answer, when we analyse her psychology closely. She herself wrote this thought, which alone would give us seriously to think: ' Oh, of course it is very painful to be unable to breathe; but it is far more so to be tortured by interior sufferings. That is terrible.' We might ask whether there be here some question of mysterious temptations. We know that in the last two or three days of her life she was tempted by the devil, but in a general way; we have no indication that she was assailed by scruples, doubts against faith, temptations to blasphemy or despair, fear of eternal damnation, such as not infrequently torment the purest of mystical souls. In what, then, consisted Bernadette's hard trial during her religious life? We must have recourse to the evidence of the most reliable witnesses.

Mother Henry Fabre, who became novice mistress and, later on, secretary to the Superior-General, Mother Marie-Thérèse Vauzou, attests: ' Sister Marie-Bernard *suffered much* from the behaviour of Mother Marie-Thérèse Vauzou; but if she cried sometimes she never complained.' Be it noted, once for all, that these depositions, made on oath during the Canonization Process, are not ordinarily suspect of exaggeration. The religious who are giving their evidence before the commission of examiners, nominated by the Bishop, weigh their words and, fearing to fail in charity towards their sisters in religion, are inclined rather to say less than the truth than to go beyond it.

Sister Valentine Gleyrose, an intelligent and

virtuous nun, a former superior, and during the last years of her life employed in the secretariate of the Mother-House, said of Bernadette that ' she was often seen to be sad, and to cry sometimes, without ever complaining.' So during ten years as a religious, Bernadette lived frequently, if not permanently, in a state of sadness, that cast a shadow over her life, and even sometimes drew tears from her, although she had been brought up hardly and maintained heroic silence and courage.

Mother Bordenave, who was secretary to Mother Marie-Thérèse Vauzou, and subsequently Superior-General of the institute, who has written what is unquestionably one of the best biographies of Bernadette, also attests at the Process: ' In order to have borne this trial, the Venerable Servant of God must have needed *great strength of soul*. She had to endure a long and slow *moral martyrdom*.'

As the reader will recognize, if he will weigh carefully this evidence, given after reflection by one peculiarly authorized to speak, there is here no question of just a simple expression that is not to be taken literally. If it were merely a way of speaking, Bernadette would not have required a great strength of soul. Moreover, we shall find this expression, ' moral martyrdom ' used repeatedly. We are told again, for instance, that certain of Sister Marie-Bernard's fellow religious, ' thinking they were carrying out the wishes of Superiors,' contributed their share to *the moral martyrdom* which the Saint underwent. Again, we read in the report of the Process: ' Sister Marie-Bernard was the object of humiliations which not only made her suffer mentally but were *a martyrdom for her heart*. It is added that ' she must have possessed a hope carried to the point of heroism, for her trust in God not to have been shattered.'

Let us note again that what is here in question is a ' moral martyrdom,' properly speaking, and not by any means a metaphor, since there was need of a hope carried to the point of heroism in order to endure it to the end.[1]

This last attestation will enable us the better to understand the reflection of Sister Victorine, who had been ordered to look after Bernadette at the hospice at Lourdes, and cared for her devotedly from All Saints, 1861, until her departure for Nevers in 1866. ' When she learnt of the death of the Venerable Servant of God,' testifies Sister Marcelline Durand, ' the first thing she did was to thank God, for she feared lest Bernadette might end by becoming discouraged.' And perhaps leave the Congregation !

The fact, then, that Bernadette had to bear a very heavy and prolonged trial in the convent of Nevers cannot be seriously and impartially controverted; we can only discuss the manner of it. Whilst endeavouring to attenuate rather than exaggerate the responsibility of those concerned, let us try to fix precisely in what this trial consisted and by whom it was caused. Bernadette was fond of reading the Lives of the Saints. ' She regretted that their defects were not sufficiently made known to us.' She was right, a hundred times over ! One of the greatest

[1] Before entering upon the account of the sufferings that Bernadette endured from certain of her sisters in religion, we think it our duty to insist upon the truth that these religious were pleasing to God. Our Lord said to St. Margaret Mary : '' I do you much honour, my dear daughter, in making use of such noble instruments to crucify you. . . . I am using in your case persons who are devoted and consecrated to me.'' (*Vie de Sainte Marguerite-Marie*, published by the monastery of Paray-le-Monial, p. 126.) St. Margaret Mary was, then, crucified by her sisters. Bernadette was not crucified by her sisters, and the reputation of her community, more so than that of Paray, remains essentially intact and safe.

mistakes in hagiography is that we are not sufficiently informed either with respect to the defects of the saints or the defects of those who surrounded them, and made them suffer.   Thus there has been eliminated from the true story just what might have been most edifying and instructive for souls anxious to attain to perfection.

A first question might be asked, and we own to having envisaged it as very probable. Having studied the spirit of the religious institutes in the latter half of the nineteenth century, we have been forced to conclude that they were enjoying a period of great prosperity at the close of the Second Empire. The greater number of the teaching congregations had built fine houses, where, as was fitting, they endeavoured to impart a superior education, especially to the young girls of the well-to-do middle class. Accomplishments were greatly appreciated and, as a natural consequence, so also were the exterior gifts possessed by certain pupils. To impress the families of the pupils, entertainments were organized, which ended in the chapel with vocal items of sacred music inspired quite as much by profane as by religious art. Obviously a Bernadette Subirous, dropped into such a milieu as this, even though highly esteemed doubtless on account of the apparitions of our Lady, must have been but little considered otherwise; since as regards her state and her exterior qualities she was an insignificant personage who, at first sight, showed no sign of her great moral value.

In 1895, twenty years after Bernadette's death, the chaplain of the Mother-House was describing the impressions of deep faith and religious enthusiasm with which he had returned from a pilgrimage to Lourdes, and paid a visit to Mother Marie-Thérèse Vauzou, then Superior-General. The latter asked

him: 'You are then convinced of the truth of the
occurrences at Lourdes?' 'Certainly, Mother,' replied the priest, and he went on to speak of the
miracles that had recently taken place there, of the
incredible number of pilgrims who were arriving
there, led by their priests and bishops. Nor did he
omit to mention the liturgical Office of the Apparitions, which had been approved by the Holy See.
The Superior cut him short in a very decided tone:
'If the Blessed Virgin,' she observed, 'willed to
appear anywhere on earth, why should she choose
an uncouth, ignorant peasant girl, instead of an
educated, virtuous and distinguished nun?' This
was not, as might be thought, a sudden retort which
had occurred to her and to which the Superior
attached no importance, but in her case it was a
very decided opinion. The same Mother Marie-
Thérèse Vauzou said to Mother Bordenave, then her
secretary: 'Oh, Bernadette was a little peasant. I
do not understand how the Blessed Virgin could
have revealed herself to her. There are so many
others, so refined, so well brought up. However!'
    Thus, then, twenty years after the death of Sister
Marie-Bernard, she who had been her novice mistress,
and later Superior-General, maintained as a sort of
fixed idea that our Lady could not have appeared to
Bernadette because she was not sufficiently distinguished. Here we see an example of what class
prejudices can do, even in the case of fervent and
highly gifted religious. By birth Mother Marie-
Thérèse Vauzou belonged to a good, provincial,
middle-class family, and it was especially in this class,
still more than among the nobility, that the gifts and
graces due to birth were excessively and exclusively
appreciated, particularly during the second half of
the nineteenth century. Bernadette did not belong

to a good middle-class family; hence she could not have been the choice of the Immaculate Conception!

This insurmountable prejudice is all the more astonishing in the case of a nun otherwise unquestionably outstanding, seeing that the whole history of Christianity seems to be a flagrant protest against these class prejudices. The celebrated words of St. Paul, in his first Epistle to the Corinthians, will ever remain true:

See your vocation, brethren, that there are not many wise according to the flesh, not many mighty, not many noble. But the foolish things of the world hath God chosen, that he may confound the wise: and the weak things of the world hath God chosen, that he may confound the strong. And the base things of the world and the things that are contemptible, hath God chosen: and things that are not, that he might bring to nought things that are.[1]

Let us repeat that it is almost incomprehensible that after such teaching, illustrated in Church history by such startling examples, any nuns should have been unable to rid themselves of this prejudice, imbibed in their environment from their earliest years, that the Mother of God could not have chosen a child of humble rank to carry out one of the highest of missions.

Let us hasten to emphasize that these social prejudices, so unconscious and so invincible, were in no wise to be blamed upon the community at Nevers. On the contrary, that institute was one of those which had escaped most from the snobbery that flourished in educational establishments. We have already noticed, and we insist upon the point, that the Sisters of Nevers practise an edifying charity with respect to one another; they are all treated as equals, and know nothing of special privileges among themselves. The

[1] I Cor. i. 26-28.

Nevers convent, which is the Mother-House of an institute numbering two thousand religious, is, no doubt, a conspicuous building, imposing in its dimensions, in its cloisters; but the whole edifice, as also the chapel, has been designed and built in accordance with the true religious spirit, and all superfluous ornament has been excluded.   Likewise, the community rooms, parlours, etc., show immediately at first sight that, as far as possible, and more than in many other communities, holy poverty has been observed.   The atmosphere of simplicity and recollection that prevails there is truly that of the Congregation, so that in living there Bernadette did not find herself at all out of her element.   The wide family spirit, and deeply-rooted piety maintained by the Superiors and Sisters was quite specially suited to her, so that our Lady made no mistake in preferring to lead Bernadette to the Sisters of Nevers.   If she there suffered morally, it was owing to certain individuals, of whom the principal, and almost the only one responsible, was Mother Marie-Thérèse Vauzou.   The other religious in general, on the contrary, greatly helped and loved her.

In order to analyse adequately the moral martyrdom from which Sister Marie-Bernard suffered so cruelly during her life at Nevers, it is important to show how affectionate she was beneath a somewhat reserved exterior.   It might have been her weak side, and it was there that she had to be most tested.   In the course of her revelations, our Lady herself had put Bernadette on her guard against this danger of an affection carried to the point of attachment, which might have been an obstacle to a greater love of God. We have noticed earlier that Bernadette was fond of amusing herself with one of her cousins, who was also her godfather.   He died prematurely at Lyons, and

Bernadette said at the time to her confidante, Jeanne Védère: ' I knew he would not live long. I had been told not to be so much attached to him, because he would soon die.' There is no doubt that it was Our Lady of Lourdes who had warned Bernadette ' not to be so much attached ' to one whom she was led by nature to love in too human a fashion.

The fact was that Bernadette was capable of inspiring unusual affection, and she herself would have responded to it by giving herself with all her heart's strength. When she was at the Lourdes hospice, a religious named Sister Marie had been violently attached to her. ' Provided I am near her, I am happy ! ' She spent whole nights at Bernadette's bedside; she would rise quietly and seat herself beside her. As soon as Bernadette noticed this, she said to her: ' Sister, I beg of you to go to bed. I do not need you, and it disturbs me to see you there. Do go, for charity's sake ! ' Sister Marie went, but she returned a moment afterwards, and when Bernadette awoke the little scene began again. Jeanne Védère pointed out to Sister Marie that she was tiring Bernadette instead of doing her good, but the religious replied: ' What would you have? Provided I can touch her pillow, I am happy, and I do not feel the need of rest.' Jeanne also tells us that Bernadette was likewise very fond of this Sister. She who was to become Sister Gertrude declared to Sister Marie: ' I believe that God will not leave you here long; you are too much attached to Bernadette.' Shortly afterwards, indeed, this presentiment was to be realized.[1]

[1] Though doubtless a little natural, Sister Marie's attachment to Bernadette seems very pardonable and even, let us say it, admirable. Here we have a nun capable of divining the Saint's fine qualities, which proves once more that to understand the saints we must love much.

Very reserved as a rule, Bernadette sometimes surrendered herself eagerly to virtuous persons who greatly attracted her. When the wife of Admiral Bruat came to Lourdes she was accompanied by a Sister of Bon Secours, named Sister Antonine. ' As soon as she noticed me,' this religious writes in her memoirs, ' Bernadette threw herself into my arms, and showed great affection for me. I have never forgotten the expression with which she looked at me.'

Consequently, the great danger for Sister Marie-Bernard when she donned the habit of the Sisters of Nevers was much less that she would allow herself to be tempted by vanity and vainglory than that, unknown to herself, and under the most specious pretexts, she would be carried away by a passionate and absorbing affection. This danger was all the greater because she seemed outwardly more cold and reserved. Those Sisters in religion who knew her intimately were far from unaware of her great capacity for loving. ' She was faithful in her friendships,' states one of them. When the religious with whom she had had affectionate relations returned to the Mother-House, she was happy to show them marks of friendship. And if this testimony does not seem very convincing, here is that of Sister Martha Durais, which will at once enlighten the psychologist as to this side of Bernadette. She was one of those rare people who love deeply and not lightly, but who remain unshakably faithful notwithstanding disappointments, once they have given their affection. In that, she resembled St. Teresa the Great, who could declare: ' My heart is so faithful that when I have once loved anyone, I love forever.' Sister Martha Durais tells us: ' She did not waste her affection, but when she had given it, she never took it back. Speaking for myself, I have been the constant recipient of her friendship. I kept it until her death and, I hope, in the world beyond.'

Now, when Bernadette entered the noviciate of the convent of Nevers, the oldest and most clear-sighted of the community would have foretold that the visionary of Lourdes would become personally attached to her novice mistress, and nothing might have seemed more legitimate.

The said novice mistress, Mother Marie-Thérèse Vauzou, was an exceptionally outstanding person. She was about forty years of age; from both the physical and moral points of view, she was in the full possession of all her valuable and brilliant qualities. The daughter and grand-daughter of lawyers, she had been well educated at the boarding schools of Brive and Cahors, both kept by the Sisters of Nevers, and had finished her studies at Limoges. Having entered religion with the Sisters of Nevers, at nineteen she had been sent as a mistress to the Normal School at Montpellier.[1] At twenty-one, she had been placed in charge of a foundation at Bordeaux, and had finally been appointed novice mistress at the Mother-House at the age of twenty-six. This office she was to hold for about twenty years. Subsequently, she became Superior-General of the Congregation and remained such for another twenty years. It may be said that she ruled the Mother-House of Nevers and the whole Congregation during forty years. She died at Lourdes in 1907, at the age of eighty-two. It was this woman, gifted above the ordinary, to whom Bernadette seemed destined to be attracted, and who, partly unknowingly, was to make her suffer throughout her religious life.

We must enter upon a rather more detailed

---

[1] Training College for elementary teachers.

analysis of the character of Mother Marie-Thérèse Vauzou, and in order to do so we have procured evidence that cannot be gainsaid : that of Mother Bordenave, who knew her under all circumstances and at very close quarters ; having been with her eleven years at the Mother-House, and lived with her as her secretary, enjoying her intimate confidence, for six years. Furthermore, the testimony of Mother Bordenave, a very highly esteemed religious, is confirmed at every point by the evidence of Mother Josephine Forestier and of Mother Henry Fabre, who succeeded Mother Marie-Thérèse Vauzou as mistress of novices and subsequently became Assistant-General. Finally, we have the testimony of certain priests or religious, one of whom was the nephew of Canon Febvre, the convent chaplain.

The great, unusual, and almost extraordinary qualities possessed by Mother Marie-Thérèse Vauzou cannot be called in question. All the witnesses are unanimous in recognizing them. We are told that she was possessed of ability of a high order, a very upright character, and a heart of gold, one of the most affectionate one could imagine. ' Beneath a cold exterior, she had a heart that needed to give and also to receive much affection.' She had within her that mysterious and hidden gift met with in certain outstanding women, and particularly in certain nuns, of drawing hearts to her. ' There was in her,' writes Mother Bordenave, ' something like a magnetic attraction. People either feared her greatly or loved her greatly. Her behaviour was such that she could cause others either much happiness or much suffering.' Mother Josephine Forestier declares likewise : ' She exercised a kind of fascination over us, and we were very fond of her.'

Nor let us think that Mother Marie-Thérèse

Vauzou possessed only superior qualities of mind and heart. She was undoubtedly pious; she had a truly living faith, her devotion was sincere, she ardently loved the interior life, she was passionately zealous for the salvation of souls, and for their sanctification. We are assured that she joined 'piety of a high order to a very intense interior life.'

How then, it will be asked, could it be that so eminent a religious, and one so highly endowed by nature, did not understand Bernadette and caused her to suffer? We shall be told: 'It was a mystery; God permitted it.' This we are far from denying, but the mystery is not wholly inexplicable for, if God allows saints to suffer from the defects of those who surround them, these defects and faults are not for that reason any the less defects and faults! Now, according to the statement of Fr. Le Cerf, Mother Marie-Thérèse Vauzou had the defects of her great qualities. Her temperament was domineering, her mind rather severely practical. 'She had little liking for mystical states.' When she was novice mistress, she insisted above all upon 'that suppleness and trustful, gracious submission which her imperious nature greatly appreciated.' This limitation alone would already suffice to make us dread clashes between Mother Vauzou and Bernadette which would be very painful for the latter. But the novice mistress had other imperfections.

We have already cited that very important observation of St. John of the Cross, to which we think it our duty to return because it is so much forgotten: persons consecrated in religion, very pious in their manners and eminently gifted, may, without knowing it, have also great defects; the defects of their qualities. If, indeed, by dint of self-examination, by distrust of themselves and working at themselves, by submitting to the direction given them, these persons succeed in learning of and ridding themselves of these faults, inhering almost fatally to their good qualities, they will become saints. Now it is never contested in the least, by any of the witnesses, that Mother Marie-Thérèse Vauzou was not a saint. Very intelligent, very quick, she had too much confidence in her own judgement. She was too sure of herself. 'Without her being aware of it, her judgement at times suffered from the influence of her very great impressionability. This impression was lasting. It was impossible to make her change her mind and,' states Mother Bordenave, ' one did not even try ! ' She formed opinions with respect to certain persons that were premature and final ; she was absolute and obstinate in her judgements. We are told that she was unaware of the influences under which she lay, and which were the result of her temperament and upbringing. This explains how she could never allow, as we have already seen, that the Blessed Virgin could have revealed herself to a little peasant girl. Finally, in order to be complete, for although we do not wish to exaggerate neither do we wish to water down the truth, Mother Marie-Thérèse Vauzou was rather liable to take offence easily.

Because the Superior-General, Mother Josephine Imbert, used from time to time to speak confidentially to Mother Eleanor Cassagnes, the Assistant-General, the mistress of novices felt some resentment and even antipathy to the latter. 'I have wondered, moreover,' remarks Mother Josephine Forestier, ' whether, given the nature of Mother Marie-Thérèse Vauzou, the presence of Bernadette, the object of such notoriety in the religious world, did not grate upon her.' ' Mother Marie - Thérèse Vauzou,' attests Sister Marcelline Durand, ' did not like privileged souls,

and was always seeking to depreciate them.   It was
a matter of temperament in her case.'

How regrettable it was that this nun, so remarkably
gifted, had not closely examined and studied herself,
and so had remained unaware of her faults !   Such
as she was, with her capabilities and her deplorable
failings, she exercised an immense prestige, a prepon-
derating influence in the institute of the Sisters of
Nevers.   Beyond all question, she contributed to
make of Bernadette a great saint, for during the years
the latter spent at Nevers Mother Marie-Thérèse
Vauzou, though only the novice mistress, owing to
her influence over Mother Josephine Imbert, the
Superior-General, who was then ill, and to her
intellectual and moral qualities, was virtually the
effective superior of the Mother-House, and even of
the entire Congregation.

CHAPTER X

THE INTERIOR SUFFERINGS OF SISTER MARIE-BERNARD

WHEN Mother Marie-Thérèse Vauzou, the novice mistress, learnt of the forthcoming arrival of Bernadette at the convent of Nevers, she rightly considered it as a special grace which the Blessed Virgin had reserved for the Congregation. She was personally highly honoured in being entrusted with the training of this novice, already celebrated throughout Christendom. She was aware of the responsibility that she was assuming. She wrote: 'You will understand what a grace and privilege it is for us to receive the favoured child of Mary. For me it will be one of the greatest joys of my life to see the eyes that have seen our Lady.'

On her side, with her simplicity and generosity, Bernadette eagerly surrendered herself to her novice mistress, and this very lively affection ought to have lasted always. At first, it was even somewhat excessive, and the novice soon realized that she must moderate it. In all the biographies of Bernadette, the authors rightly mention this fact, apparently of small importance, but which reveals a state of soul: Mother Marie-Thérèse was returning to the convent of Nevers after an absence of some days. The novices were awaiting her in the cloisters, to receive her and greet her affectionately. As soon as Sister Marie-Bernard saw her appear, without casting a thought to the impression she might give and the opinions the other novices might exchange, she was the first to throw herself into the arms of the mistress. Another religious, who was assisting the latter, remarked subsequently to Bernadette: 'What an outburst, Sister Marie-Bernard!' 'Oh, yes,' replied the novice, 'it was far too natural, was it not? I was very sorry for it afterwards.'

This incident, which happened during Bernadette's first year at Nevers, clearly shows us that the novice loved Mother Marie-Thérèse dearly, even passionately, and that she was persuaded that the mistress returned her affection. If, indeed, Sister Marie-Bernard had been instinctively aware of some coldness between her mistress and herself, she would not have been the first to literally throw herself into her arms.

Two months after her arrival, one evening in the absence of Sister Marie-Bernard, Mother Marie-Thérèse Vauzou told the novices that they were highly favoured in looking upon the eyes that had beheld the Mother of God. 'Watch,' she bade them, 'when Bernadette looks up to heaven. Those eyes shine with a light that is quite heavenly.' Evidently at this period the novice mistress fully believed in the apparitions. Moreover, she was very attentive to the novice, who was so privileged and whose health was so precarious. About five months after she entered the noviciate, Sister Marie-Bernard was worse. 'During some months which I spent with her in the infirmary,' states a fellow novice, 'I noticed that the mistress of novices showed herself rather well-disposed towards her, and came to see her every day.' Everything, then, leads us to believe that in the early days Mother Marie-Thérèse felt kindly towards Bernadette, and in return the latter showed her much affection. Even when the feelings of the mistress had changed towards her, when she treated her with a harshness that astonished the novices all the more in that the mistress had never treated one of them so rigorously, Bernadette withdrew none of her affection, being intimately persuaded that Mother Marie-Thérèse acted thus entirely from motives of duty and charity. It was then that she answered Sister Bernard Dalias, who enquired whether she were not hurt at the mistress's behaviour: ' Oh no ! She is right to act like that, for I am very proud.'

It is true that, when she reprimanded Sister Marie-Bernard in season and out of season, Mother Marie-Thérèse quite believed, and not without reason, that she was acting from motives of duty and virtue. It is not necessary, however, to be very closely acquainted with the life of religious of both sexes to know that, too often, behind the most supernatural motives, there are hidden sympathies and antipathies that are not supernatural, but are inspired by temperament, by the personal preferences and the instinctive and unsuspected aversions of nature. Mother Bordenave attests during the Process of Canonization: ' Mother Marie-Thérèse Vauzou justified to her own conscience —which was upright and very delicate—the excessive severity which she meted out to Sister Marie-Bernard by the necessity of humbling the latter on account of her outstanding mission, but it is certain that she did not like Bernadette. When she spoke to me of the Venerable Servant of God, I could not discover any sign of kindly feeling for the latter.'

This was a deeply-seated antipathy, and precisely for that reason, it was unknown to the novice mistress, and so irremediable. ' She herself had no idea of the prejudice under which she laboured.' The dislike she felt for Bernadette led her, throughout her life, to doubt the miraculous occurrences at Lourdes. Being the novice mistress, she inclined the Superior-General, Mother Josephine Imbert, to doubt them also. ' One day, she said to me, with a slightly pensive air : " After all, the rose bush did not flower." '

It will be remarked that, since Sister Marie-Bernard was only a little more than a year in the noviciate and subject to the authority of Mother Marie-Thérèse, she had not to suffer very long, but we have already said that the religious in question was virtually the Superior of the Mother-House, so that Bernadette had to endure her coldness and general behaviour throughout the years she spent at Nevers.

Two years before her death, as a result of the progress of the tuberculosis, Sister Marie-Bernard developed a swelling on the right knee, which caused her to suffer greatly, forced her to remain in bed, and when she walked to do so with crutches. ' On a painful occasion,' relates Sister Marcelline Durand, ' Sister Marie-Bernard, suffering from a tumour on her knee, met Mother Marie-Thérèse, who addressed some sharp words to her. Bernadette gave a sigh. " Oh, our mistress ! " as though to say : " She is always after me ! " Then Mother Marie-Thérèse rejoined : " Ah ! we have touched her self-love ! " ' Here again, we have one of those significant little incidents for which Taine sought, and which convey so much. At this stage, Sister Marie-Bernard had no longer any illusions, and she had long known that Mother Vauzou had no longer the slightest liking for her. She was ill, in a pitiable state, dragging herself along the cloisters with difficulty. Mother Marie-Thérèse never let pass an occasion of wounding her to the quick by some cutting word. We learn from the Process that Sister Marie-Bernard's simple reply, ' Oh, our mistress ! ' astonished and almost scandalized the religious who accompanied Mother Marie-Thérèse. Yet for ten years the sick nun had

ceased to be a novice, and according to the Constitutions was no longer under her in any way. Only the
mistress, by that mysterious ascendancy which we
have mentioned, inspired a veritable cultus on the
part of the majority of the religious who loved and
venerated her. Bernadette, on the other hand, was
considered an ignoramus, a useless member of the
community, though one whose virtues could not be
denied. 'She was,' they repeated after Mother
Vauzou, ' a good, ordinary religious.'

Let us not be afraid to insist upon this fact, for it
is typical and the situation must have occurred often.
Mother Marie-Thérèse excused herself by saying:
' Ah ! we have hurt her self-love.' Was it really
self-love that she had hurt; and was it her business
to do so? Ought she not, rather, to have spoken a
few pleasant and encouraging words to the invalid,
who for the time being was a little better? In our
opinion, it was the heart she had hurt rather than the
self-love of the poor sufferer who, thanks to one of
those efforts she was in the habit of making, had
come out of the infirmary for a little walk.

And now, let us imagine Bernadette who, as we
are repeatedly informed, was particularly fond of
Mother Marie-Thérèse Vauzou, and perhaps cared
for her all the more in proportion as she was less
liked by her. She saw the religious whom the mistress
kept about her, whom she loaded with marks of
favour, and made ' very happy.' Notwithstanding all
her virtue, when she returned to bed, Sister Marie-
Bernard could not but have thought that, weak and
ill as she was, she would have been glad to have
received a kind word; ' one of those drops of comfort,'
as Sister Teresa of the Child Jesus called them. It
was rarely oil and wine that Mother Marie-Thérèse
Vauzou and Mother Josephine Imbert poured into

her wounds; it was nearly always water mixed with a little vinegar. 'Whenever I spoke to Sister Marie-Bernard,' confessed Mother Marie-Thérèse after the death of the latter, 'I always felt moved to do so sharply.'

We shall understand better the remark made by Mother Valentine Gleyrose: 'I was painfully impressed by the manner in which Mother Marie-Thérèse Vauzou treated Sister Marie-Bernard. I considered it wrong.' A number of the community shared this opinion, but there were others, partisans of the powerful novice mistress, who considered that the latter was quite right, since she could do no wrong. 'Some of Sister Marie-Bernard's companions respected her, but believing they were entering into the views of the Superiors, they usually concealed these feelings in the depths of their hearts. Nay more, there were those,' states Mother Bordenave, 'who contributed their part to the moral martyrdom which Sister Marie-Bernard endured.'

This expression 'moral martyrdom' which recurs so frequently, and reminds us of that other somewhat longer one: 'a long and slow moral martyrdom,' which Sister Marie-Bernard must have borne with 'great strength of soul,' 'with heroism,' must be clearly explained and understood.

In the institute of the Sisters of Nevers, Bernadette was not made to suffer at all in material things. She was never, as has happened in the cases of other saints, deprived of care, remedies, or of the food required in her state of health, both as to quantity and quality. As has been rightly pointed out, she received consideration. The Superior-General sometimes took her out for a drive, and never spared necessary expense in her regard. All the suffering endured by Bernadette, and which she felt cruelly, consisted in the manner in which the two Superiors behaved to her; and outward behaviour matters much, and is even essentially important in the case of an invalid who is being greatly tried and is very sensitive. We are not indulging in conjectures, more or less probable; all our allegations are based upon the documents. The Sisters in the kitchen, wholly taken up with their household duties, are less understanding in the matter of delicate feeling. We know how one of these caused pain to St. Teresa of the Child Jesus, and a similar incident occurred in the case of Bernadette. The cook, we are told, who had never been ill, did not always understand the little thoughtful attentions necessary for the sick. When she was ill, Bernadette found a difficulty in taking the food that was served to her, and the infirmarian asked for something lighter for her. The cook retorted: 'Perhaps her mother used to give her chicken every day?' This speech was repeated to Bernadette, who remarked: 'It is true, but what Mother did give me she gave so willingly!' The said Sister-cook repented of this speech during her last illness and said: 'Oh, if the time were to come over again!'

Bernadette's words express her feelings. So far as her malady allowed, she was not difficult in matters of food, but she was extremely sensitive and, above all, she longed for things to be given her with a good grace. She agreed with the author of the Canticle of Canticles: 'If a man should give all the substance of his house for love, he shall despise it as nothing.'[1] Consequently, from this standpoint the important question is less to know that her superiors did not deprive her of what she needed, than to know the manner in which they gave her these necessities.

[1] viii. 7.

Did they do so cordially, or did they frequently show
indifference or coldness? Seemingly, this distinction
matters little, especially in the case of healthy folk,
engaged in active employments, who find distractions
and compensation in their daily occupations. But it
is a very different matter for a nun who never goes
out of her convent, who is unable to fill any useful
position, has nothing to distract her thoughts, is
frequently confined to a bed of suffering, spends her
nights sitting up and breathing with difficulty, and
has time to feel at length the reaction from the moral
wounds inflicted upon her. The smallest unkindness
from those she loves, and from whom she might rightly
expect some comfort, constitute a veritable martyrdom
when frequently repeated.[1]

These wounds were frequent in Bernadette's
religious life, but their causes were so slight, they
seem so insignificant, that they have not been dwelt
upon and handed down to us. Certain unkind
remarks, however, have been passed on. ' On a
certain occasion,' we are informed, ' Mother Marie-
Thérèse said to Bernadette : " Now we can slap you ! "
Bernadette replied resignedly : " I hope, Very Reverend
Mother, that you will do so gently." In the institute
of the Sisters of Nevers, they were pleased and proud
to possess her who had seen the Immaculate Mother,
and been the principal human cause of the most
frequented of pilgrimages. Mother Vauzou knew it,
and would have been very upset if, on account of her,
Bernadette had returned to her family, but Sister
Marie-Bernard was resigned, patient and virtuous.
She had made her vows, and, moreover, she felt too
surely that she was in her place among the Sisters of

[1] This daily suffering, which we have tried to define precisely,
fully justifies the remark of Cardinal Verdier : ' Hidden behind her
convent walls, amid trials of all sorts, the humble Bernadette had, as it
were, to win pardon for the glorious privileges she had received.'

Nevers to consider going elsewhere.   Hence, Mother Marie-Thérèse was able to say: 'Now we have you, we can slap you!'

However, this last incident must not be taken too seriously.   The novice mistress had not the least formal and avowed intention of 'slapping' Bernadette, nor did she do so in the strict sense of the word, but we should note well that often expressions and words escape us which, though we know it not, come from the depths of our being, and contain an important element of truth.   It is devoutly to be wished that after uttering these words, and hearing Sister Marie-Bernard's meek reply, Mother Marie-Thérèse had gone and knelt before the Blessed Sacrament, and thoroughly and conscientiously examined herself as to the secret movements underlying her behaviour. This examination of conscience might have been of decisive importance in the case of the novice mistress who, as we have said, was otherwise pious and eminently capable.   If, after having prayed and examined herself, she had gone to Bernadette's bedside, spoken kindly to her, and told her not to attach any importance to what she had said; if she had taken her some little dainty and, what would have been worth still more, promised that thenceforth she would show her real, sisterly friendship, she would have poured balm into the wounds of the sick nun, and carried out one of those acts of charity which are so pleasing to God that they cover a multitude of sins.

Instead of making this humble, thorough, sincere examination of conscience, Mother Marie-Thérèse Vauzou remained as she had long been towards Bernadette: cold, distant, unsympathetic.   Although we may not have exact details to quote, what we have related is sufficient to enable us to understand, without either exaggerating or attenuating, what was the meaning of this attestation of Mother Bordenave, which sums up in a few words the long trial of Sister Marie-Bernard : ' Throughout her religious life, and without showing any outward sign, she endured treatment that *wounded* her, on the part of Mother Marie-Thérèse and Mother Josephine Imbert, the Superior-General.'

Here is one example among many others of this kind of behaviour. 'During a retreat,' says Sister Gonzaga Campy, ' I was awaiting my turn at the door of Mother Marie-Thérèse Vauzou's room. The bell rang for the conference. I had to go and, seeing that I was losing my turn, I felt rather impatient. I had been waiting for two days. Sister Marie-Bernard, who was on her way to the conference, approached and touched me on the shoulder, saying : " There is someone giving way to impatience." I turned round to her and said : " But there, I have been waiting two days ! " With a gesture of indifference, she replied : " Ah ! That does not matter ! " '

Sister Marie-Bernard was accustomed to such trying treatment; she had learnt to submit to even less legitimate trials of obedience, and she could give advice; but she had not acquired this imperturbable patience without experiencing interior motions of rebellion, and that was why she so often accused herself of pride. It is harder than might be thought in the world to be humble and patient when, in a religious community where everything ought to be done according to equity and charity, subjects are made aware that, in practice, others are specially privileged who are unworthy of being thus favoured, and abuse the favours or the interviews with the Superior which they themselves can scarcely ever obtain.

An important question may now be asked : What

was the chief reason why Mother Marie-Thérèse Vauzou did not retain towards Bernadette that sympathy which is necessary for understanding a soul? Though it may seem complex, this problem is not difficult to solve. The novice mistress, all-powerful over the Superior-General, was an imperious woman. As we have said, she possessed one of those autocratic characters which cannot endure that a soul, even one who is loved, should submit by halves. By instinct, such characters wish to have entire possession, and when they come up against an immovable obstacle they break, and their love changes to antipathy. Mother Josephine Forestier, who was very fond of Mother Vauzou, related that in her capacity of private secretary, she had much to suffer from the latter's temperament, particularly during her first years of office. 'When I knew her better, I humbly made the advances, flinging my arms round her neck, so that her coldness ceased for the moment; but such a procedure was not always successful. Did Bernadette understand that it was necessary to act thus? She did not dare to make the advances which we made, who saw Mother Marie-Thérèse at closer quarters.' Above all else, the mistress desired that they should give her their entire spiritual confidence; she liked the nuns, we are told, and appreciated their piety according to the confidences she received upon their interior life.

We have frequently remarked that Bernadette was not at all given to speaking of such confidential matters, nor could she analyse and explain her spiritual states. Moreover, she had to guard jealously the secrets entrusted to her by our Lady, and which concerned her interior life. If only, with our Lady's permission, she could have revealed those secrets to Mother Marie-Thérèse, and to her alone, the novice mistress would have taken no account of the differences in their upbringing which separated them, and would have petted and shielded Bernadette. But then, Sister Marie-Bernard, who had, as Mother Henry Fabre tells us, ' a capacity for loving very ardently,' would have been in danger of becoming too much attached to Mother Marie-Thérèse, who knew how to make herself loved by her novices.

We desire, above all, to be impartial and just. When Mother Marie-Thérèse summed up in a few words Bernadette's defects of character, ' Character: inflexible and very sensitive,' she was not absolutely wrong. Neither by nature nor by training did Bernadette possess the flexibility of the religious who flung their arms around Mother Vauzou's neck, and always made the first advances. There had been impressed upon her, as is often the case among the simple folk, a rather too rigid and narrow conception of justice and truth, that prevented her, even on the pretext of charity, from voluntarily expressing any sentiments which she did not feel naturally. In her private notebook, she accuses herself of being excessively easily hurt, and considers that her dominant fault. Now, when she was severe, Mother Marie-Thérèse shut up souls. From a scruple and also from want of flexibility, Bernadette did not know how to adapt herself to the character of her Superior.

The dislike which the latter bore her lasted all her life and persisted after her death. The former novice mistress, who had become Superior-General, held to this final opinion: ' Bernadette was a good ordinary religious.' It was as if photographed upon her mind, we are told. ' Even after the cures attributed to the intercession of Sister Marie-Bernard,' attests Mother Bordenave, ' she did not modify her opinion. She never told me one word of those cures, and I learnt of them only when, in my office of private secretary, I had charge of the archives, and then found the letters referring to them. So strong was the impression in her case, that it was impossible for her to control it and, furthermore, she was unaware of it.' She said again: 'As for what concerns the Canonization of Sister Marie-Bernard, wait until after I am dead.'

She was convinced that Bernadette's movements of impatience could not be reconciled with sanctity. Here again, we willingly recognize that the quick, sharp rejoinders of Bernadette, when she was worn out with pain and grievously tried, were imperfections for which she humbled herself, and for which she was less responsible than she believed. Sister Joseph Garnier, who witnessed these sometimes violent sallies on the nun's part, said: 'You see, with all her visions, she is like other people!' Such was the opinion of the religious who were wholly devoted to Mother Marie-Thérèse. Fr. Le Cerf states during the Process: 'It was Mother Henry Fabre, I believe, who told me that sometimes, in presence of the manifestations of the crowds at the grotto, which she could watch from the windows of her room, Mother Marie-Thérèse, towards the close of her life, used to become unnerved, and close the shutters quickly.'

We need not attach too much importance to this statement, since, after all, it was Mother Marie-Thérèse herself who, in 1883, had caused to be constructed the Lourdes grotto which we may see to-day at the entrance to the convent of Saint Gildard at Nevers. She wished to thank the Blessed Virgin for the cure of her secretary, Mother Josephine Forestier. Nevertheless, the erection of this grotto, dedicated as a kind of *ex voto* to our Lady, is not a convincing proof of the Superior's personal devotion to Our Lady of

Lourdes.   The evidence of witnesses that she scarcely believed in the apparitions is too abundant, and they are too completely in agreement.   For instance, Fr. Le Cerf tells us: ' She attached little importance to Lourdes, nevertheless Providence called her to die there.'   Three nuns who were members of her council said, likewise, about 1895, to a priest who was astounded at this lack of credence: ' Then you do not know that our venerated Mother is not inclined to believe in the occurrences at Lourdes?'

Mother Marie-Thérèse Vauzou had a great devotion to our Lady, and she was also an excellent business woman.   She had judged it very opportune to have a grotto erected in the grounds of Saint Gildard, and in this she was not mistaken; but, none the less, she retained her prejudices against Bernadette. ' Whilst I was talking to her,' we are told by the nephew of Canon Febvre, the chaplain to the community, ' I felt that she was prejudiced against Sister Marie-Bernard, and I verified the fact that she did not share that high opinion of her which had led my uncle to propose the latter as a model of religious life.'

At the close of her life, Mother Marie-Thérèse felt that her conscience was not tranquil with respect to the conduct she had observed towards Sister Marie-Bernard.   ' I was afraid,' she said, ' lest I had been too severe in her regard, and that was tormenting me.' She went to the Cistercian abbey of Fontfroide, in order to consult an excellent monk, Père Jean, who bore a great reputation for sanctity.   She interviewed him alone in the parlour, and then followed him into the confessional.   When leaving the monastery, she confided to her secretary: ' I am quite at ease now. I explained why I had acted as I did and Père Jean has quite reassured me.'   Two months before her death, she said again to Mother Henry Fabre: 'God permitted that Mother Josephine (Imbert) and I should be severe with Sister Marie-Bernard in order to keep her humble.'[1]

The large element of truth contained in these assertions must not prevent us from recognizing the erroneous element which they may also contain. It is greatly to be desired that religious could convince themselves, once for all, of this elementary theological truth: The fact that God may permit a certain line of conduct on the part of Superiors in no way justifies that conduct; for, once more, God does permit, very often and even generally in the case of Superiors, defects and faults from which the subjects may profit by submitting themselves and practising patience. Mother Marie-Thérèse Vauzou had explained to Père Jean, in all good faith, the motives which, in her eyes, justified her conduct, and the good Father had reassured her, as was his duty, and as any religious might have done.[2]

[1] She added: 'What struck me in Sister Marie-Bernard was her detachment from the world; her lack of self-interest, which made her always refuse what was offered her for herself or her family; the precision in her account of the apparitions which I heard several times, and of which she never altered a word. That always seemed to me the supernatural side of that child, as did also her expression, which had something heavenly about it. On the natural side, one could see self-love.' Seemingly, in the last days of her life Mother Marie-Thérèse may have believed in the visions, for she said that the protection granted by God to the Congregation was due, among other causes, 'to the love of which the Blessed Virgin has given us proof in sending us her privileged child.'

[2] Père Jean Léonard, Prior of Fontfroide, and later its first Abbot, was born in 1815, of peasant stock, at Valbourne, in Languedoc. He became a priest, and subsequently Rector of the Seminary of Nîmes, and later entered the new Cistercian Congregation of Sénanque. Though noted for great personal piety and austerity, more than one incident of his career would incline neutral readers to doubt of his discretion in matters of spiritual direction, especially when nuns were in question, and his reassurance of the Superior-General does not carry entire conviction. (Tr.)

We began by pointing out that the 'long and slow martyrdom' which Bernadette bore so heroically was especially, and almost exclusively, the work of the novice mistress and the Superior-General. It is pleasant to recognize that many of the community esteemed and loved Bernadette, lightened her burden, and even rendered life in the convent agreeable to her. The annals of Saint Gildard frequently allude to Bernadette in very appreciative terms. We should mention one, very particularly, Mother Eleanor Cassagnes, who remained at the Mother-House throughout the lifetime of Sister Marie-Bernard. 'Of all the nuns of the Congregation whom I knew,' attests Mother Josephine Forestier, 'she was the one who has left with me the strongest impression of sanctity. She was Sister Marie-Bernard's counsellor, support, confidante and, as it were, guardian angel.' This high praise enables us to see in Mother Eleanor Cassagnes a living model of what the Sisters of Nevers ought to be. Moreover, many of them resembled the charitable Mother Eleanor Cassagnes rather than Mother Marie-Thérèse Vauzou.

Hello, whom Henri Bremond not unfairly called 'a minor prophet,' was exceedingly fond of this short formula: 'To understand means to equal.' It is quite true that to understand another implies a certain equality or conformity of outlook, thoughts and experience. Mother Eleanor Cassagnes perfectly understood Bernadette, and was, it may be said, her only and faithful confidante. Consequently, when we are told that no member of the Congregation gave so strong an impression of sanctity as did she, we have no difficulty in believing the assertion. Let us wish that those who perfectly understood the trials and the inexhaustible patience of Bernadette may be many. 'Sister Marie-Bernard faced the obstacles in her religious life with unfailing humility, and a generous and silent acceptance, and in order to obtain divine help, she made use of humble and trustful prayer.' So states Mother Bordenave. We must now see precisely in what consisted this humble and trustful prayer.

CHAPTER XI

SPECIAL DEVOTIONS OF BERNADETTE IN HER LAST YEARS

AFTER having undergone the experience of her religious life, Bernadette gave utterance to this deeply thoughtful reflection, which conclusively reveals for us her state of soul: 'From my point of view, the creature will never be more than an instrument of which our Lord makes use in order to make me suffer. . . . For love of Him, I will carry the cross hidden in my heart bravely and generously.'

She constantly prayed to our Lady for help to carry out this resolution faithfully, and never to attach herself to anything created, be it what it might. The sufferings which she encountered in her religious life, and which have been shown in the preceding chapter, constrained her, so to speak, to become more passionately attached to our Lord. As a result, she came to feel the need of a close and intimate union with the divine Master. 'I am convinced,' attests Mother Bordenave, ' that the more she became aware of antagonism on the part of creatures, the more she cast herself into the arms of God.'

The disappointments, loneliness, unforeseen infidelities which we suffer unexpectedly on the part of men are supremely profitable if we know how to turn from them to God. They strengthen our faith, purify and increase our love. If Bernadette had been surrounded with affection by Mother Marie-Thérèse Vauzou, to whom she was much attached, she would have been too humanly happy in the cloister, and without realizing it she would have let herself become lukewarm in a too mild atmosphere.   No doubt she would have remained a good religious, faithful to her rules, present in choir, communicating piously, making the Way of the Cross from time to time; but without the trial, without the continual moral suffering, she would have been satisfied with an ordinary, good Christian life.

On the contrary, we have shown how all her life she suffered inwardly from the coldness and positive unkindness of a Superior whom she liked, and as a consequence felt so much the more keenly the need of turning to God.   Hence she clung with all her strength to Jesus crucified, as the ivy clings to the oak.   Some reflections or thoughts which she wrote in her notebook show us how heavy was the burden, and how strongly she clung to our Lord.   We may be allowed to quote verbatim some of these notes. Had she copied and partly composed them?   We do not know.   What is certain is that she had intimately assimilated them, and made them her daily spiritual food.   Moreover, they are prayers as much as thoughts, and in order to understand them fully the reader must think them over slowly and repeat them.

'Oh, Jesus, forsaken and, at the same time, the refuge of those who are forsaken, Thy love is teaching me that it is from Thy loneliness that I must draw all the strength I need to bear mine.   I am convinced that the most terrible loneliness into which I could fall would be to have no part in Thine; but, by Thy desolation, Thou hast merited that my heavenly

Father should not abandon me; and that He should never be nearer to me by His mercy than when I am most closely united to Thee, O Lord, by loneliness.

'I beseech Thee, O my God, by Thy loneliness, not to spare me but not to abandon me.   In affliction, teach me to see Thee everywhere, as my only comforter.   Give me grace to recognize Thy hand in it, and not to desire any comforter but Thyself.'

These thoughts were written by Sister Marie-Bernard in the year 1873, at a time when she was very sorely tried, and allude to a desolation that may have been due to several causes, but of which we have discovered one of the chief.   It was at that time that Sister Eleanor Cassagnes surrounded her with care, and comforted her amidst the trials she had to endure from Mother Marie-Thérèse.   She had also found it useful to write down her resolutions and the best prayers she read and composed, so as to be able to find them again when she needed them.   The years 1873 and 1874, during which, at more or less lengthy intervals, she composed her precious private notes, were a period of interior struggle.   Fairly often, she turns to our Blessed Lady as her advocate.

'O most holy Mother of my Lord, who hast seen and felt the loneliness of thy dear Son, help me now in mine !   And you, saints of Paradise, who have passed through this trial, have compassion on me who suffer it, and obtain me the grace to be faithful unto death.'

The interior suffering of Sister Marie-Bernard led her spontaneously, and by a supernatural inspiration, to seek all her strength and consolation in the love of Jesus suffering, and, consequently, in His Sacred Heart.   The first pages of her book of spiritual notes are already eloquent in this respect.   She writes:

' Why have I come here, if not to love our Lord with my whole heart, and to prove my love for him? Following His example, I must suffer and sacrifice everything to Him generously. Courage, my soul! Prayer obtains everything; the Heart of Jesus is here; let us knock!'

Here is a thought to which a lukewarm and indifferent person would doubtless attach little importance, but which a tried, fervent soul, longing after holiness, will thoroughly understand and even try to put into practice daily: 'O Jesus and Mary, grant that at last all my consolation in this world may be to love you and to suffer for sinners. O my God, give me to comprehend the holy jealousy of divine love; detach me, draw me to Thyself, and uplift all my affections.' Here we see Bernadette setting herself with all her might to refine her love, and to give her heart exclusively to God.

We have suggested that by force of circumstances, and by the Spirit of God, Bernadette had been led to unite herself to the Sacred Humanity of Jesus and to His Sacred Heart. We might now cite some very convincing extracts, but we have a still more decisive proof, and one that is absolutely incontestable, of her devotion to the Sacred Heart. We have been told repeatedly that Sister Marie-Bernard was fond of reading the lives of the saints. Doubtless her spiritual intuition, which acted like a divine instinct, led her to read the life of St. Margaret Mary. There she found a love of suffering that encouraged her to bear her own, and an intensely ardent devotion to Jesus Crucified that made one and the same thing with the love of the Sacred Heart; for we must never forget that St. Margaret Mary saw the Sacred Heart in vision surrounded with a crown of thorns and surmounted by a cross.

'My God,' the Saint writes, 'granted me this grace, namely that He would never be wanting to me. For my whole life was spent amidst bodily sufferings, due to my frequent illnesses and continual weakness, whilst my spirit endured derelictions, loneliness amidst the contradictions and humiliations of creatures. . . . My divine Master willed that I should suffer everything in silence, and bade me take this motto:

> 'I will suffer all without complaint,[1]
> For my pure love casts out all fear.'

Bernadette, no less than St. Margaret Mary, had spent her whole life amid bodily suffering, and in continual infirmities, whilst her heart had endured desolation, loneliness and humiliation. Her soul found in the great Saint of the Sacred Heart a sister, an exemplar and a rival. After having read the motto assigned by our Lord to St. Margaret Mary, forthwith Sister Marie-Bernard copied it out and adopted it with one slight modification. She wrote in her notebook:

> 'I will sacrifice all and suffer all without complaint, since Jesus casts out all fear.'

Why did Bernadette replace the two words, 'pure love,' by the simple name 'Jesus?' No doubt, she feared to take to herself that expression 'pure love,' feeling that she was still too imperfect, and in her humility not thinking in the least that her love was sufficiently purified. Whatever it may have been, the motto 'I will sacrifice all and suffer all'

---

[1] *Vie de Sainte Marguerite-Marie par elle-même*, Paray-le-Monial, p. 129.

explains now more clearly than ever how Mother Henry Fabre could say: ' Sister Marie-Bernard suffered much owing to the behaviour of Mother Marie-Thérèse Vauzou; but if she cried sometimes, she never complained.'

If the motto borrowed from the biography of St. Margaret Mary were the only quotation in Bernadette's book, it might be objected that it did not prove much, but there are others more convincing and conclusive. Led by extraordinary ways, St. Margaret Mary found herself faced with the criticisms of her Sisters and Superiors. She derived great joy from these contradictions, and although enduring bodily pain also, she could write:

> ' The more my love shall suffer from their blame,
> So much the fiercer burns that one consuming flame.
> Though men afflict me night and day,
> They cannot tear Him from my soul away.
> The greater anguish my poor heart may know,
> The closer will He knit me to His Heart here below.'

Sister Marie-Bernard, who throughout her religious life endured misunderstandings and trials, immediately seized upon these lines, and wrote in her notebook:

> ' The more my love shall suffer from their blame,
> So much the fiercer burns that one consuming flame.
> Though men afflict me night and day,
> They cannot tear Him from my soul away.
> The greater anguish my poor heart may know,
> The closer shall I knit me to His Heart here below.'

It can be seen that the copy is exact. The text is that of St. Margaret Mary, except for a slight altera-tion in the last line.

The Saint who did so much to spread abroad the devotion of the Sacred Heart offered an example of a special privilege that could not but strike and attract Sister Marie-Bernard. In her autobiography, St. Margaret Mary writes that our Lord told her: 'I wish to give you My Heart, but you must first sur-render yourself as a victim to be sacrificed.' This special vocation to vicarious sacrifice had predestined St. Margaret Mary to find in creatures no longer anything but occasions of contradiction, humiliation and opposition. Our Lord willed that these should be as ' her delicious food.' After Holy Communion, the Saint had asked of the divine Master ' never to allow anything to befall her but what might cause her the most humiliation and abjection in the sight of creatures, and to destroy her in their estimation.' Sister Marie-Bernard wrote:

' *M. M. Victim.*

' I desired that they should no longer remember me, save to despise me, humble and insult me; since nothing else indeed was my due.'

Was this reflection Bernadette's own, or did she copy it from some biography or pious book? We do not know, but there seems no doubt that the first letters and the word, *M. M. Victim*, stand for *Margaret Mary*, *Victim*. In any case, the thought perfectly expresses that thirst to be despised which is repeatedly found in the life and revelations of St. Margaret Mary.

This particular devotion which Sister Marie-Bernard bore to the Sacred Heart will surprise us less if we go back in imagination to the period, and recall the national Vow which, after the war of 1870, had been officially formulated in the name of the whole of France, to build in reparation a basilica at Montmartre. Again, in Bernadette's notebook, from the first, and almost on every page, we find thoughts and prayers mentioning the devotion. She writes: ' May my crucified heart be forever buried in Thine, and hidden in the mysterious wound opened therein by the spear ! '

' Oh, most pitiful Heart of Jesus, accept every one of my tears, every cry of pain, as a supplication for all those who mourn, and for those who forget Thee ! '

These invocations of a loving soul that offers its sufferings for its suffering or unfaithful brethren might be attributed to St. Margaret Mary. When Bernadette copied them, she at least made them her own, in order the better to carry out her vocation to sacrifice. It would be superfluous to multiply such. Sometimes, however, she seems to think only of uniting herself to the Heart of Jesus, especially when she feels most sorely tried:

' Jesus, I am suffering, and I love Thee. I am suffering, and my sighs are rising to Thee, my Redeemer, without ceasing. It is in Thy adorable Heart that I am shedding my tears; it is to It that I am confiding my anguish; my bitterness to its bitterness. Grant, O Lord, that they may be sanctified by this holy union.'

' O Mary, my Mother, take my heart and bury it deep in the Heart of Jesus ! '

During the greater part of her religious life, Sister Marie-Bernard had as her director Fr. Douce, a Marist, who was chaplain to Saint Gildard.[1] This holy religious encouraged her in her devotion to the

---

[1] Père Douce was chaplain to the convent of Saint Gildard until October, 1876, and was then replaced by the Abbé Febvre.

Sacred Heart, and in her loving suffering for the salvation of sinners.   It was under his guidance that her soul made its dwelling in the Hearts of Jesus and Mary.   She wrote: ' The Heart of Jesus, with all its treasures, belongs to me.   There I will live and die, in peace amidst sufferings.'

' P.D.   (Père Douce).   " Place yourself in the Heart of Mary, and stay there.   Make it your home on earth."   O Mother, it is in your heart that I will lay down my heart's anguish, and thence I will draw strength and courage.'

Hence Bernadette's fervent devotion to the Sacred Heart seems beyond doubt, and, directly or indirectly, it drew its inspiration from St. Margaret Mary.   Let us remind ourselves again that the latter's devotion thereto was one with her devotion to the Passion and to Jesus crucified.   Often this is forgotten.   From the time of the first revelations, or visions, which prepared that Saint for her extraordinary mission, she spent her nights at the feet of Jesus Crucified.   Later on, throwing herself at the foot of her crucifix, she said to Him: ' O my dear Saviour, how happy I should be if Thou wouldst imprint in me the likeness of Thy sufferings ! '

Let us not be surprised, therefore, that the cultus of the Sacred Heart led Bernadette, also, to the cultus of the Cross.   We shall see, in fact, that her love towards Jesus Crucified will develop in such wise that her devotion to the crucifix will become almost exclusive; so that in the last analysis Bernadette's supernatural life is characterized above all by her love of the Cross.   She writes, still in the notebook, this prayer, which is one of those most deeply significant of her interior life:

' O Jesus ! keep me beneath the standard of the Cross.   May the crucifix be not only before my eyes, and on my breast, but in my heart, living within me. O God, may I be myself this living crucifix transformed into Him by the union of the Holy Eucharist, by meditation upon His life, upon the innermost dispositions of His Heart; drawing souls not to me but to Him, from the height of that Cross where in this life His love may forever fix me.'

Although we may rightly criticize the literary form of this aspiration, so far as its content is concerned it is no less magnanimous and profound, and gives us the key to the whole spirituality of Sister Marie-Bernard.[1] In fact, if we continually bear in mind that from the time of the apparitions Bernadette had been supernaturally called to do penance, to suffer in all kinds of ways, to imitate Christ crucified; to become, as she herself says, ' a living crucifix,' for the salvation of souls, we shall have no further difficulty in understanding her mission and her line of thought. She had never lost sight of her vocation to vicarious sacrifice, and when she was in the convent her director, Père Douce, seeing her at close quarters, understood her mission perfectly and never ceased to remind her of it. Once he said to her in confession: ' Remember often those words which our Lady spoke to you, "Penance! Penance! Penance!" You must be the first to put them into practice, and in order to do so bear in silence everything you have to put up with from your companions and your Superiors, in order that Jesus and Mary may be glorified. Ask our Lord earnestly to make you understand the cross

---

[1] It is well to remember that Bernadette was fourteen when she began to learn French, and that for her it was almost a foreign language. She always found spelling difficult, and though she learnt to write and speak remarkably well, all things considered, faults of grammar and style remained, and also a limited vocabulary which accounts for the frequent use of pious *clichés*, constantly found in the devotional books of the period.   (Tr.)

He wills you to carry this year, and carry it lovingly, faithfully, and generously.'

On the other hand, as we may see from the remarkable quotation above, she drew the strength she needed from Holy Communion. It may even be said that she remained always in union with our Lord in the Blessed Sacrament. Père Douce, whose advice she was exceptionally faithful in following, urgently recommended this pious practice. 'Do not be afraid. *Keep always very close to our Lord in His tabernacle*, and, following His example, carry the cross hidden in your heart bravely and generously.' These recommendations she followed to the letter, and, in order not to forget them, wrote them down at once. It is evident that she possessed an intense interior life.

We have said, what is moreover self-evident, that her continuous and painful infirmities, her moral sufferings, her trials, led and even forced her to cling the more closely to the Cross. She sought consolation in the wounds of her Lord; His humiliations; His crucifixion. 'O Jesus, Jesus,' she cried, 'I no longer feel my cross when I think of Thine!'

It was, then, the love of the Cross that continually strengthened her and brought her peace and calm, even when she was suffering most acutely. 'I no longer live a moment,' she writes, 'without spending it in loving Him. . . . O Mary, my good Mother, grant that, following your example, I may be generous in making the sacrifices which our Lord asks of me during my life. Jesus came on earth to be my model. After His example, I want to follow Him and tread generously in His steps.'

Like all mystics, Sister Marie-Bernard reached

the stage when she could suffer not only peacefully but joyously. The Sisters who visited her in the infirmary were astonished at her childlike cheerfulness. She wrote herself, after these moments of consolation: 'The Christian life does not consist only of combats and trials, it has also its consolations; and if from Thabor we must go to Calvary, from Calvary we return to Thabor with Jesus. The soul comes away from Golgotha to seek strength and courage on Thabor. There is a foretaste of heaven.'

In her hours of supernatural joy, Bernadette united herself to the elect and the angels, and repeated those lines written in her private book:

'Love triumphs, love enjoys,
The love of the Sacred Heart rejoices.' [1]

But she was already very experienced, and she knew that here below in the spiritual life the hours of gladness are only brief, bright intervals, during which it behoves us to prepare for new and harder trials. So thoroughly had she grasped this, that she prayed God to console her only in order to render her more capable of bearing the hardest sufferings for the conversion of sinners. 'O Jesus, console me only that I may suffer more, and persevere to the end in suffering. Thou, who art the light of my soul, enlighten my inward eyes in time of tribulation; and because suffering is profitable to me, take no account of my fears or my weakness. . . . Glorify Thyself in my weakness, O Lord, Thou who art my soul's only refuge.'

To suffer, in order to 'fill up what is wanting to the Passion of Christ,' in order to become, in some sense, 'another Christ'; such was the ideal—we

---

[1] No reader familiar with the life of St. Margaret Mary will mistake these lines, which are taken from her autobiography, p. 149.

might even say in a good sense ' the fixed idea '—of Bernadette, especially at the end of her life. Accustomed to repress the slightest natural repugnances, she would exclaim: ' How foolish to fall back upon self, when our Lord asks for one of our hands to nail it ! Henceforth, the more I am crucified, the more I shall rejoice.' Truly, she reached the culminating point of sanctity, and the stage of constantly practising this resolution ! Often she would say, as an ejaculatory prayer: ' O Lord, I love Thee ! Crucify me as much as Thou wilt.'

She was then confined to the infirmary, and she exhorted the younger patients to conform themselves wholly to Christ crucified. Sister Casimir Callery states: ' When I was a postulant, I was in the infirmary where she was. One night, being unable to sleep, I was restlessly turning in bed when she noticed me, and said: " When you are in bed, you should lie still and think how you are like our Lord on the cross." ' The Sister correctly concluded that Bernadette herself acted thus, for during sleepless nights she tried, by her thoughts, her love and, as far as possible, in her body, to be conformable to our Lord crucified.[1]

One of her fellow religious, who witnessed her wonderful courage during paroxysms of coughing, haemorrhages and attacks of suffocation, heard her utter only the Holy Name, without ever making a complaint. ' When she said: " My Jesus ! " ' attests the witness, ' she looked at her crucifix, and there

---

[1] After the lines borrowed from St. Margaret Mary and quoted above, we have : ' During the night, being unable to lie any longer on my left side, I wanted to turn over for some relief, Jesus said these words to me : that when He was carrying His Cross, He did not change it from side to side to ease the pain.' (*Vie de Sainte Marguerite-Marie*, p. 28.) Is there simply a coincidence between the practices of the two saints, or did Bernadette wish to imitate what she had read and admired ?

was something indefinable in her eyes. I was so edified that I could not help exclaiming, "She is a saint!"' The Sisters who came to visit her in the infirmary, seeing for themselves how supernaturally she bore her sufferings, remarked that she was ' on the Cross,' and Sister Marie-Bernard would take up her crucifix and, showing it, say: 'I am like Him.'

When her bodily and mental sufferings were at their worst, she would stretch out her arms crosswise, saying: 'Jesus, I love Thee!' Canon Auguste Perreau, who visited her during her last days, and at times when she was tortured physically and morally, attests: 'What encouraged her was, above all, her love for Jesus crucified and for the crucifix.'

We shall end this chapter with a consideration which seems to us as important as it is encouraging. We have drawn attention to several points of resemblance between St. Bernadette and St. Margaret Mary. They differ from each other, however, in a particularly noteworthy feature of their devotion. It is true that both had a great love for the Heart of Jesus pierced with the lance, but as we have seen, and shall see again, Bernadette was drawn rather to the crucifix. But the most essential difference between the two saints lies in the paths which they followed. Mother Marie-Thérèse Vauzou was not wrong when she frequently repeated: ' Sister Marie-Bernard is a good ordinary religious.' The chaplain of Saint Gildard, Père Douce, himself, said—although he held a very high opinion of Bernadette—' She is an ordinary, good religious.' The fact was that after the apparitions at Lourdes, and particularly after she entered religion, Bernadette had no longer been favoured with visions, revelations, or extraordinary graces. In her devotions, and in her penances, she avoided all singularity and in these matters was in no way different from her companions. Even more than did St. Teresa of Lisieux, she walked by the ordinary and normal way of perfection, but that has not hindered her from attaining to the highest sanctity. Of her, as of other saints who have followed the common way in everything, it may be said that she carried out the most ordinary duties of the religious life with an extraordinary perfection. Let us add that the exemplary life led by St. Bernadette, her daily efforts to correct herself of her smallest imperfections, such as her impatience, her steady endeavour to keep the thought of Christ crucified before her—wherein she found her strength—are more imitable and quite as admirable as the visions and favours enjoyed by St. Margaret Mary. In the case of Bernadette, we find words, prayers and example that are within our reach and which, with the grace of God, we may easily imitate.

There is an oft quoted thought of the little Saint which is, indeed, one of her most noteworthy, and which any Christian might frequently repeat with great profit and make a rule of life:

' My divine Bridegroom has given me an attraction for His humble and hidden life, and He has often told me that my heart would never have rest until it had sacrificed everything to Him. And to make me decide, He often inspired me with the thought that, after all, at death I shall have no comforter save Jesus and Him crucified. I shall carry into my grave, in my icy fingers, Him who is my sole faithful Friend. What supreme folly it is to attach myself to anything but to Him!'

The time was not far off when, before she died, Bernadette would go through such physical and moral agony that she would be unable to have any comforter save Jesus and Him crucified.   As she had said, Him alone would she carry to the grave in her icy fingers.   Him, her sole faithful Friend !

CHAPTER XII

THE DEATH OF BERNADETTE

THE death of Bernadette, like that of every saint, comes to confirm the heroic virtues which she has particularly practised. If we had not already pointed them out in previous chapters, it would reveal the specific characteristics of her piety.

During her continual sufferings, she had clung to Jesus crucified, as her Consoler. In 1877, she made the effort to send a letter to the Superior of the boarding school at Cahors, who had offered her a large crucifix. She wrote: 'For a long time I have wished for a large crucifix to put near my bed. How can I thank you enough? Whilst I held it and kissed it, I exclaimed that my dear Mother Sophie had been happily inspired. I have leave to keep it and I am happier with my crucifix, on my bed, than a queen on her throne.' In its simplicity, this exclamation expresses one of the noblest thoughts ever voiced by the Christian mystics. We shall not find St. Margaret Mary or St. Teresa of Lisieux voicing a more sublime or magnanimous cry than this. This sovereign happiness which the sick nun declares she derives from contemplating our Lord on the Cross might seem startling. The fact was that during the last year of her life Bernadette was enduring physical torture. We have seen that an enormous tumour had formed in the right knee, and cramp had supervened which rendered the leg extremely sensitive.

Her pain was so violent that it seemed as though it would imperil her life, and her face was becoming cadaverous. She passed sleepless nights, and if she dozed off for a short time sharper attacks of pain would wake her suddenly. She could not prevent nature from uttering involuntary complaints and cries, but as soon as she recovered full consciousness and self-control, she would humbly ask pardon of the nuns nursing her and repeat: ' My God, I offer it to You! My God, I love You.' [1]

Her condition became worse, and during entire nights she could no longer sleep or doze. Acute pain forced her to moan so continually that her fellow patients in the infirmary could not sleep. After these terrible attacks, she would say: ' Oh, I do beg your pardon for complaining so much.' Tuberculosis was destroying her whole frame, and she became so thin that her flesh seemed reduced to nothing and it looked as though the bones must be exposed.

In February 1879 her condition further deteriorated and left no longer any hope of recovery. She was obviously hastening rapidly to her end; death was drawing nigh, and it was merely a question of days. They had begun to sit up with her every night. Bernadette was in bed, but she had her right leg out of bed and resting on a chair. The nights were very bad, with uninterrupted moaning. A novice who was sitting up with her at this stage could not sleep for a moment. Sister Marie-Bernard noticed this, and in the morning told the infirmarian:

[1] The different accounts of the witnesses for the Canonization Process do not seem to us to agree as to the dates of the minor details ; but it matters little, since our object is to emphasize what is characteristic of Bernadette's spirituality, and from this point of view the documents cannot be gainsaid. Moreover, we do not claim to relate everything.

'I do not want that Sister to watch me. I want Sisters who sleep. She has not slept. If I need anything, I can call them.'

During March, the malady, a kind of galloping consumption, made frightening progress. The nun who was watching beside her was obliged to change the position of the poor patient, who could no longer do anything for herself, and called the infirmarian to help her. 'The latter,' she says, 'made me climb on to a chair at the head of the bed to raise the patient. We realized the atrocious pain Bernadette was enduring to find a bearable position on an air cushion which she was using. Her poor body was just one wound, and she was indeed terribly thin, and said herself: "Oh, if you could only find something in your pharmacy to ease my back! I am all flayed."'

A little incident took place, apparently unimportant, but which in view of what we have said regarding Sister Marie-Bernard's spirituality, seems very significant. 'The patient,' attests the Sister Secretary, 'made them remove all the pictures which they had previously fixed to her bed to satisfy her devotion; as they asked the reason for this wish, she pointed to the crucifix and said: "He suffices me."' Thus, in her last days, and at the moment when she entered upon her last agony, Bernadette wanted nothing whatever to distract her from our Lord. One might have expected that the visionary of Massabieille would have asked them to place before her eyes a picture of Our Lady of Lourdes. The detail reveals much. During her last days, St. Teresa of the Child Jesus had made them hang a picture of the Holy Face on her bed curtains: 'Oh, how it has helped me!' she exclaimed after one of her most painful nights. Bernadette, suffering as

much as she, and dying of a similar malady, desired
no longer to unite herself to anything but the crucifix.

The fever that had for so long been undermining
her had vanquished her at last. ' The poor child
had always shown herself very energetic in her
suffering,' we are told; ' now she felt overcome by
the disease.' The only part of her body that was not
yet affected, and even seemed to revive most strik-
ingly, was her sight. ' Her eyes,' writes the Abbé
Febvre, ' always bright and clear, took upon them a
more remarkable expression. We were impressed by
it, above all when she gazed fixedly upon her crucifix.
They even became more expressive as her body
became more feeble.' In this connection, the priest
remarks: ' It seemed as though death were respecting
the eyes which, during the apparitions, had beheld
the Immaculate Conception.'

On the Friday before Passion Sunday, March 28,
it was decided to give her the Last Sacraments, and
she received them about three o'clock. When the
Superior-General entered, Bernadette said, in a very
strong voice that amazed everyone: ' Dear Mother,
I earnestly ask pardon for all the trouble I have
given you, and for all my faults against the Rule;
and of my dear Sisters for the disedification I have
given them, especially by my pride.'

Bernadette was so convinced of her supposed
worthlessness, that she had rallied all her strength to
make this kind of public confession. The Superior-
General remarks: ' This was said in a tone of such
conviction that we were *taken aback*. The voice
was *thunderous*, like that of a preacher who wants
to make himself heard by all his congregation.'
Much moved, the Sisters maintained an impressive
silence. Hearing her speak thus loudly, the Superior-
General felt reassured as to her condition, and shortly

afterwards said to the religious: 'Then she is not so bad.'

On Easter Day, someone had said to her: 'You will rise again with our Lord and savour the joys of Easter,' but she had replied: 'My passion will last until my death.'

Next day, on her bed of suffering, very weary, her face purple, she said to her Sisters: 'I am being ground as a grain of wheat!' She was draining the chalice of pain to the dregs.

On Wednesday in Easter week, the day of her death, she was sitting in an armchair, breathing with difficulty and suffering dreadfully; beside her, they were saying the Prayers for the Dying. In a weak but distinct voice, she repeated all the acts suggested to her. 'Above all,' says the chaplain, 'it was not without emotion that, from time to time, we saw her open her eyes eagerly, and cast a look of supplication and love to the crucifix hanging on the wall close to her armchair. The Superior-General said to the dying nun: 'Dear Sister, you are on the Cross at this moment.' She stretched her arms crosswise whilst looking at the crucifix, to render herself more like our Lord, and replied: 'Jesus! Oh, how I love Him!'

Once more, the Abbé Febvre spoke to Bernadette, exhorting her to have confidence, and reminding her of the words of Holy Scripture, which call upon the bride of Christ crucified to place Him as a seal, or as a bundle of myrrh, upon her heart. 'Suddenly,' says the chaplain, 'we saw her take up a crucifix and place it on her heart, clasping it firmly. She wanted it to remain there, so it was fastened lest she should throw it off in the involuntary movements caused by her agony.'

A Sister who came in shortly afterwards asked

her: 'Sister, are you suffering much?' 'It is all good for Heaven,' was her reply. 'I am going to pray to our Lady to comfort you.' 'No,' answered Bernadette, 'not consolation but strength and patience.' So did the dying nun remain heroic up to her last moments. What courage there was in that little religious, whose body had been enduring agonies for several days!

Towards two o'clock in the afternoon, a sort of relative calm came over her, and Bernadette expressed a wish to rest. The priest went off to the chapel to hear confessions and the religious withdrew. Three-quarters of an hour later, Sister Nathalie, one of the Assistants to the Superior-General, who had just been to confession, felt urged to go up to the infirmary. As soon as she entered, Bernadette stretched out her arms to her, as though to call her to her assistance, and said: 'Help me! Help me! Pray for me!' Again, she asked for forgiveness of the Assistant for any trouble she might have given her.

One of her last gestures was again to seize the crucifix, lift it to her lips, and, slowly and devoutly, kiss the five wounds of the Saviour. She no longer thought of anything save of the Passion, and of identifying herself with our Lord. She said: 'I am thirsty.' She made the Sign of the Cross as only she could make it, and then distinctly recited the last words of the *Ave Maria*. 'Holy Mary, Mother of God,' but instead of saying, 'pray for us,' she implored, 'pray for me a poor sinner, a poor sinner,' and finished, 'now, and at the hour of my death!' After these final words, an attack of suffocation stopped all breathing; she bent her head, and expired. It was about three o'clock in the afternoon.

Bernadette died very humbly, imploring the divine

mercy up to the last moment, still more for her own sins than for those of other sinners. None the less, she was one of the purest victims that this earth has known, dying on the Cross after the example of her divine Master.

In the history of the Blessed and the Saints, a singular phenomenon has occurred fairly frequently. Servants of God whose virtue has passed unnoticed all through their lives have, on the day of their death, been proclaimed saints by the multitude, and honoured with a kind of cultus.

The virtues of Bernadette had not been unrecognized by her Sisters; far from it, but when the general public learnt of her death, it felt moved to come and show its religious veneration beside her mortal remains. Further, as a result of some special grace, though wasted and worn out by illness, the body of Sister Marie-Bernard seemed to be re-clothed with a supernatural beauty. 'We saw her body,' writes the Secretary to the Superior-General, ' as it were revive. Not only did the traces of suffering disappear from her face, but the terrible emaciation sensibly diminished. Her expression was calm and rested, and those who watched her closely never tired of gazing upon her. During three days, her limbs remained perfectly flexible, and her hands retained their natural colour. The finger ends were even rosy, as though the blood were circulating through them.

The Bishop of Nevers, Mgr. Lelong, wished the body of Bernadette to be exposed in the convent chapel. In her hands, she held a crucifix, and on her head was a crown of white roses. A numerous throng began to file past this body, which looked like that of a young and small girl. Nobody had any doubt that she was a saint! The temperature was close and it was pouring with rain, yet they waited a long time. 'We could not see her when she was alive,' said someone, 'we will see her dead.' Soldiers were particularly noticed among the crowd, and were the most anxious to touch her body with pious objects, as they would a relic. An officer asked: 'Sister, could you let me have some medals?' The Sister had none, so he went off into the town, and returned with a package of medals which he had bought. Everyone wanted to have a souvenir that had touched the dead. Four or five religious were charged with this task, and the Nevers shop-keepers had never sold such a quantity of pious objects. For three days the body lay exposed.

On Saturday, April 19, the park almost opposite the convent was crowded with people. The Requiem Mass was celebrated at ten o'clock by the Archpriest of the cathedral, and the Bishop had interrupted a round of Confirmations to come and pay homage to the favourite of Our Lady of Lourdes. He was surrounded by his Vicars-General, the cathedral Canons, and by clergy of the town and neighbourhood. Fr. Sempé, Superior of the Missionaries of Lourdes, and the Abbé Pomian, chaplain to the hospice, and Bernadette's first confessor, were there. M. Henri Lasserre, author of the book, *Our Lady of Lourdes*, was among the layfolk. The cathedral choir sang the Mass. Children's voices became this funeral ceremony, carried out with unusual solemnity in honour of Bernadette. After Mass, Mgr. Lelong preached an eloquent panegyric of her whom the voice of the people was canonizing before the Church had spoken. He then gave the Absolution, and the procession was formed to carry the deceased to her last resting place. 'It was,' so we are told, 'a veritable triumphal march; a radiant sun had followed the rain, and shone upon the terraces and trees of the garden. The long files of religious, priests and laity, wound through the paths, whilst a crowd was massed on the esplanades and convent terraces. The body of Bernadette was laid in a very beautiful Gothic chapel, dedicated to St. Joseph and standing in the centre of the garden. The Bishop said the last prayers, and then, amidst an impressive silence, the nuns sang the *Salve Regina*. All joined in this prayer which the pure voices addressed to our Lady. Doubtless the soul of Bernadette had already winged its flight to heaven.

That Saturday evening, the religious and some priests gathered again in the chapel, and recited the rosary, whilst Fr. Sempé gave a public meditation on the Glorious Mysteries.

The body of Bernadette was interred in a vault constructed in the middle of the chapel of St. Joseph, and there remained, not without being venerated and working miracles to which many *ex votos* bear witness, until September 22, 1909, when Mgr. Gauthey carried out the first Recognition of the remains. It was found intact and free from all corruption. In 1925 Bernadette was beatified, and, clothed anew in the humble religious habit, her body was placed in a *chasse*, simply designed in good taste, and transferred to a chapel situated at the entrance of the convent church. It is there to-day, after the canonization, that the faithful go to venerate and invoke the Saint of Lourdes.

We know not what we should most admire in Bernadette; the extraordinary graces received at

Massabieille, which have created what is to-day the most celebrated and frequented and, beyond doubt, the most beneficent pilgrimage in Christendom; or the daily efforts which the ignorant daughter of the Subirous must have made to reach the high peaks of sanctity and accomplish her high mission of vicarious sacrifice. We have already seen, but we feel we are bound to end by repeating it, that what is most encouraging in Bernadette, what draws us to love her quite specially, and to invoke her with the greatest confidence, is that throughout her life, and especially during the thirteen years spent in the convent, unaided by revelations, ecstasies, or extraordinary graces, leaning only on the staff of the Cross, she had to climb slowly the way of sorrows to Calvary. It was by that road, and by a death in great suffering, that she reached the Thabor of perfection and Canonization.